The Dash Club

A Book To Encourage Living Life To The Fullest!

Also Written By Darrell D. Simms
"Black Experience Strategies & Tactics In The Business World"

"May I Help You Understand?"

"The Mahogany Table"

Also Published By Management Aspects Company
"For My Peoples" by Shanisse R. Howard

The Dash Club

A Book To Encourage Living Life To The Fullest!

Darrell D. Simms

Management Aspects Company
1355 S. Corrine Drive, Suite 101
Gilbert, Arizona, 85296 U.S.A.

Management Aspects Company
1355 S. Corrine Drive, Suite 101
Gilbert, Arizona, 85296 U.S.A.

This book presents material that is for informational purposes only. It is a book based on the authors opinions and personal experiences. It is sold with the understanding that the author is not engaged in rendering legal, accounting, financial or other professional services. If financial and legal advice or other expert assistance is required, the services of a competent professional should be sought.

For information address: Management Aspects Company, 1355 S. Corrine Drive, Suite 101, Gilbert, AZ 85296

ISBN 0-9630776-9-4

Reprint by arrangement with Management Aspects Company

Printed in Hong Kong, January 2006

Publisher's Cataloging-in-Publication
(Provided by Quality Books, Inc.)
    Simms, Darrell D. (Darrell Dean), 1953-
       The dash club : a book to encourage living life to
    the fullest! / Darrell D. Simms.
      p. cm.
      ISBN 0-9630776-9-4

      1. Quality of life. 2. Success. 3. Values.
    4. Spiritual life.   I. Title.

    BF637.C5S5442 2006   158
                 QBI05-600213

Visit Management Aspects Company on the World Wide Web at
http://www.managementaspects.com
Also at http://thedashclub.com

Acknowledgements

This book was written to enhance the lives of people around the World, especially in the United States of America. This is a book of motivation, encouragement and reflection.

I would like thank all of the members of the original Dash Club which was formed in Arizona in the summer of 2004. We all realized that life was way too short to miss enjoying any of it. So thanks, Dan and Dolly Larson, Bing Xu and Jiang Bo Gan, Gregg, Monica and Benjamin Kussmann, Karl Weaver, Kuor-Shin Chang, Shahin Farahani and Nazanin Darbanian, and to my life long friends Betty and Jack Morgan and my loving wife Nelda.

I want to acknowledge my brothers and sisters for their love and prayers and whom I love dearly. I thank my children Darsha and Thorin Simms whom are always a source of encouragement to me. I would like to acknowledge my newly discovered family in Maya and Mandaue on the Island of Cebu in the Philippines. You all have shown me that life keeps getting better and better.

I would like to thank my content and grammatical editor Paivi Juvonen, she is the greatest. She also did an excellent job laying out the cover. A big thank you to my graphics editor Leslie White of DP Printing for the graphics on the front cover.

Many thanks go to my final readers: Victor Berrios, Harry Gaul, Gregg Kussmann and Michelle Hardy

A final thanks goes to Pastor Chad Moore for sharing the great story and message of the Dash that help inspire the title and premise of this book.

Dedicated

To My Loving Mothers

Ellenese Brooks Simms
&
Ina Cleo Claudette Moore Simms

CONTENTS

THE DASH! 11

YOUR BIRTHDAY! 29

UNDERSTANDING HOW GOOD IT IS! 34

DO! 43

THE DASH THINKING PROCESS! 51

ON SELF! 58

PEOPLE! 65

CREATING A GREAT SUPPORT SYSTEM! 68

WORKABLE FINANCES! 79

OWNING A PIECE OF THE ROCK! 88

GAINING AND KEEPING YOUR HEALTH! 94

FOUNDED SPIRITUALITY IS A MUST! 102

ALL WORK AND NO PLAY IS
UNACCEPTABLE! 108

HOW CAN I HELP? 117

SEX, ROMANCE AND LOVE! 124

THE WORLD IS A WONDERFUL PLACE TO LIVE,
WORK AND PLAY! 130

ENHANCING YOUR DASH FOR MAXIMUM SUC-
CESS! 137

DEATHDAY! 142

DASH ASSESSMENT SURVEY 143

WHO SHOULD READ THIS BOOK?

It is amazing how we take life for granted. I remember when I was a kid I would squash a bug and feel proud. Today, I have a much harder time stepping on a bug. Just the other day a moth came into the room and started to fly around the lamp. It was very annoying and my first thought was to squash it. Then calm came over me and I changed my plan to simply capture it and then release it out of the back door. Once I opened my hand to release it, I felt as if I had done a great thing. I felt, I had preserved a life.

This book is about preserving life. Your life! My goal is to make you rethink many of the things you do from this day forward and set you on a path of great achievement: Living your life to the fullest. You might ask, what qualifies me to think that I have such great wisdom and knowledge that would lead me to offer you such great advice and my experiences. My answer is a simple one; I live a great life here in Arizona and I am writing this book to enhance the life of everyone that would dare to read it and that includes my own family and friends. For some, I hope it brings great change and great joy to your life! For others, I hope it would simply make you change one thing about the way you live that makes your life better. For those of you who are living a great life already, I hope you would take time to do what I am doing and share your ability to live this great life with others.

Life is very short no matter how long you live. It goes by very quickly no matter what you do. None of us can truly slow down or speed up time, but we do have power over the activities that fill it and the pace that we live it. We don't often value time until we find out we don't have much of it left.

I ask you to keep one thing in mind as you read this book – not one day is promised to us when we are born and we should live each day as if it were our last one. These types of thoughts and beliefs should lead us to getting the most out of each and every day of our lives. It is about believing Life truly is the most precious possession that we will ever have and it should be valued and treasured like no other person, place or thing. Now you know why you should read this book – The Dash Club!

The Dash Club

Chapter 1

THE DASH!

I was attending church one evening and a new young pastor was giving one of his first messages to the congregation. His main focus of ministry was to help the members of the congregation to get connected with other members of the church. When he first got up to speak, I went through my checklist of: is he going to be any good; can he add value to the already great pastoral staff? He started to speak and I thought his voice was not one of a great speaker and I started to write him off as not so good. Then he introduced his topic of: "Why we are here and what is our purpose in life?" The next thing he said was most profound. He asked a question that went like this, "What are you going to do with your Dash?" And then he started to qualify and explain his question.

He said, when you die, on your headstones under your name, there are three things displayed:

- The first is your birthday.
- The second is the day you die.
- And then there will be a Dash to separate the two dates.

Birthday - Deathday

In that moment he captured the congregation's attention and of course that included me. I leaned forward and listened attentively. He then proceeded to deliver a most eloquent message. (By the way he is one of my favorite speakers to day.) He said, your birthday is easy to explain and the day you die is easy to understand, but the Dash in the middle usually doesn't get an explanation. Yet, it represents every other day in between your birthday and your deathday.

The Dash is all that it takes to represent your entire life on your headstone, a simple "-". Isn't it amazing to think, that after you die, this is all that it takes to represent your entire life? Whether you live one year or a hundred years, a mere Dash will say it all!

Then he asked several more great questions, "What will your Dash represent?" Will it be something that people will think about and contemplate, such as, she lived a great life? She was a wonderful person! His contributions to the community and society will never be forgotten! Or maybe it will say, she lived a horrible and corrupt life and was a menace to society! Or, that boy should have died in his mother's womb; he was no good and rotten from the day he was born!

It doesn't matter whether you live a long and prosperous life or a short and insignificant one; the Dash on your head stone will not be any longer or shorter, except due to the font that is chosen to make it. Again, here is the question, "What will your Dash represent?"

Now stop here a minute and ponder this profound question and think about how old you are today and then think about the harder question, how long do you think you might live. Then ponder this set of harder questions: Are you enjoying your life? Is it a good life? Is it a great life? Is it an excellent life? Is it an outstanding life? If your maker said, "your time is up," would you be begging for more time or could you smile and say "Ok; I got my fair share of time on this great earth. I am ready to get out of here now."

I don't know about you, but I get chills down my back whenever I think about my personal death, but then I start to answer those other questions and I find that I am having a very good life. Oh sure, I wonder if I married the right woman (after two children and 28 years of marriage). I still wonder if I could have done anything differently to help raise my children better. I ask some proverbial questions about my career and education choices. I have some traditional, what if questions. But, after much of the pondering, I turn to God and say, "thank you for a great and wonder life." I don't think I will ever be ready to stop living, but when my time is up, I hope to have no regrets, besides it doesn't matter any way. When it is your time to go, you are going.

We should continuously ponder the questions above from every angle and as hard as it is to change how we live, we should continue to change our lives and make them better and better – the best that we can do. I am proposing that the quality of your Dash is mostly under your control and should represent the finest set of experiences that can ever be lived.

With the above premise I present, "The Dash Club." My hope is, it will enhance your life and help make your Dash represent something great and exciting about you!

"Why a club?" you ask. I always like the attributes of a club. Clubs weave threads of commonality for people. A club is a place of being and belonging and accomplishment. It sets out the amenities for all of its members to share and enjoy. It can present a set of principles for all to live by. A club presents the discipline of rules and regulations when needed.

I believe that humanity also makes up a club that we are all born into and we are a part of it no matter what we do. We may choose not to interact fully with the membership or fit into the club's structure at various times. What do I mean by "the club's structure?" I believe we all control a certain part of the Dash Club and the people nearest us are a part of our personal "Dash Club structure." I believe the club benefits afford us great amenities and I encourage you to take advantage of all them. I suggest you learn to adhere to its by-laws and follow its rules for the good of the order as oppose to compliance. I think if you can achieve full participation in the club you can enjoy life to the fullest and help the rest of the membership to maximize its enjoyment as well! How you interact within the club's structure is what this book attempts to present.

Now get on reading this book for your life awaits you. Don't you waste one more minute of your Dash without the actions items presented in this enlightening work! Now that I have given you some idea of what the benefits are of being a member of the Dash Club. I would like to describe an important tool that we will use to present actionable steps you can take to make the rest of your Dash great.

Dash Actions Explained!

Throughout the book at the end of most chapters, I will present some concrete actions you can take to really make being a member of the Dash Club a great experience. I hope you accept them in the spirit they are offered and that is to enrich your life, which is the intent of this entire book. They are only suggestions and recommendations and should not be construed as the only way to get your desired results. They will be numbered, but that does not imply that one must come before the other. Each of them should stand on their own unless otherwise stated. Please do not think of them as clinical solutions. I am not Dr. Phil or some other trained expert or clinician. I am a person who loves to write and share his thoughts and experiences in hope that it will help other people to enjoy life as much as I do. If you find them to detract from your life stop reading "The Dash Club," throw the book away and write and tell me where I went wrong. If you find them to be helpful to you, please make them a practice and write me and encourage my life and enhance my Dash. The rest of this chapter sets out to define the features and attributes of the club in more detail. We will start this discussion by first talking about what quality we might achieve for our Dash.

The Quality of Your Dash!

While traveling in Asia, I heard a saying, "a horse and a man dies the same death." And my response is, "but they don't live the same life," most of the time the man controls the life and destiny of the horse. The man usually has the option of controlling his own destiny. In the next few sections of this book I would like to focus on the attributes of our Dash that we can control. These are things such as controlling the speed of our Dash and how we might lengthen our Dash. I think the speed and length of our Dash helps make up the quality of our Dash. All together this leads to controlling a most precious gift called life. We should be the one in control of how this life unfolds and how we use our time on this earth to make the definition of the Dash clearer and as solid of line as possible in time. I am of the mind we can maximize how true and deep the quality of our Dash can be and that we not allow our lives to fade in and out as broken lines. In keeping with the analogy of the Dash being compared to a printed line, I once worked for the greatest printing company in the world, Hewlett Packard. We spent millions of research and development dollars on making sure that the characters that were printed on paper by the LaserJet was the best in the world, at all levels. Many engineers toiled many years to perfect the quality of the characters and they patented "True Fonts" for insuring the characters could transcend their shapes and sizes and could be recognized no matter what font or orientation was used. The "A" would always be recognized as an "a" no matter what its size or shape or color. I think if you think of the Dash as a character that represents your life, you want it to be a character that is well recognized. You want it to be well designed and to have all the best research and development one can give it. A Dash with qualities being long, deep, dark and well constructed that will represent a great and long life with all of its challenges, purposes and pleasures.

Again, I pose this defining question, what makes up the quality of your Dash? There should be at least the following attributes: You should have great health. You should have a great spiritual life and a belief that is founded in something greater than you – for me this is God. You should have a good relational, support structure made up of family and friends. You should have strong mental constitution that allows some really clear thinking. You should have workable finances that will stand the test of time. You should have joy in your life. Happiness should abound and if it doesn't you should do something to make it flourish. You should have peace in your life and you should seek this at all cost. Different people will have varying degrees of these attributes as presented above. You should have the best of these Dash attributes that your life can afford and you should strive to live life to the fullest. You see, you only get one Dash and you don't get to do it over, hence the topics and actions presented in this book.

The quality of life can be defined in so many different ways and can often be defined by our mistakes and successes. Yes, of course, you get to make mistakes, but mistakes should come from trying very hard to get it right. And getting it right can be as much of an iterative process as you need it to be. You should in no way be scared to make a mistake and don't make the same mistake too many times, especially if they become detrimental to the quality of the Dash. Defining this Dash is a life long process and interestingly enough you should be the one defining the quality of your Dash as long as you are in control. Once you are gone we will all take a stab at trying to put into words what we observed about your life. We will likely say things like she was a "good woman" or he was a "bad man." What I hope people will say about me is, "he spent some quality time sharing his thoughts with the world and what he shared changed a lot of people's lives for the better." I think I just wrote my epitaph, how cool. This quality of life is definitely a refining process that we will go through one step at a time as members of the Dash Club. The way I see membership in the Dash Club working is you must be committed to making each and every day as a member into a great success.

I hope the quality of your Dash is defined more by your successes rather than your mistakes. I hope you make the right mistakes to strengthen your Dash for a long, prosperous and enduring life. I hope every mistake is just a stepping stone to the next success. Once we achieve a certain level of success with in the Dash process we can start to interact with other members of the club. These members will enhance our Dash in many ways. It is fundamental that we seek to live peaceable, that we love somebody and that we be loved by somebody. If you add the health and wealth and faith to this combination, I believe you are experiencing a form of heaven right here on earth. The quality of your Dash should be enriched at every experience. The overcoming of each challenge, no matter how big they are, should move you forward in life. The key – you are in control of your destiny, unlike the horse.

The Length of Your Dash!

Our science, recent history, statistics and the bible says that Man should get about 75 to 80 years upon this earth before becoming part of the support structure for the headstone that will display your Dash. Living a long and prosperous life is not an easy task, but it is a worthy one. In the United States it is more than doable. The one thing that is important about making life work for you in the US is making sure you understand the rules of society and here is where most of the rules for the Dash Club come from, yes, good ole' society. We often call it the system that comes from cultural norms. I am one who believes we are all a part of what makes up this club as well. If you go out looking for "the system," you will likely not find it. It will often find you. Let's look at some necessities for living this life. Education, a good job, good health, a good lover and others things we need to live a long and prosperous life.

All of the things mentioned above are all available to you from the society you live in as long as you are willing to follow the rules of the system. Take education, we spend our early life trying not to get an education. As a teenager, I was about making a few dollars and having some fun and trying to get over on the system. After some positive forces came into my life namely a positive, forward thinking, cousin and a caring step mother, I figured out education was a good thing. I got the degree and haven't looked back since. Yep, the good job followed. If you take good health, I use to think I was invincible and didn't need anybody or anything to keep me well. I found, this was typical young male thinking. Once my doctor told me, "you have hypertension and you need to eat better and learned a little about cause and affect," I realized that seeing a doctor regularly and having a good diet accompanied by some good recreation, better known as exercise, was a necessity. Fortunately, I went in the Navy and became a medic and realized how vulnerable we are and how easy it was to lose your health. What about finding that good lover?

I got married at eighteen to a girl that was fourteen and realized neither one of us was old enough to get beyond the physical attraction of good sex. When the arguing started I realized it was much more about communication and I am still working on this one. All of these things will add to the length of your Dash.

The Speed of Your Dash!

I don't know about you, but when I was a young kid time went by about as slow as molasses pouring out of a bottle, maybe even slower. Today at the tender age of 50ish, time moves at warp speed. I have come to value time more than any other thing in life. I have finally learned not to push time, but to flow with it as much as I can. I try not to waste time, but to enjoy every minute of it. This leads me to learning to enjoy "processes" that lead to the results I desire out of living my life. In this case "process" is simply what steps I need to take or allow to happen to complete desired actions. I get very disturbed when people waste time, whether it is my time or theirs. Yes, theirs, if I am to value time, I have to value it at all cost. I count time as a resource that is valuable and precious. If I see some one misusing time and he or she is a part of my Dash Club structure, I will be sure to let them know in an encouraging way that they could use the time better. Remember, I care about these people as part of my family or my friends. When I think of how little time we spend on this earth it becomes more precious than anything. After all when time stops, your Dash ends. Ah huh, think about that last sentence at least twice! The Dash is made up of a starting time and an ending time and all life in between.

So when time presents itself, you should make every possible way to use it wisely and effectively. When possible, slow it down to a comfortable pace. What does it mean to slow time down? For me, it is simple; I try to think about what is happening in the moment and control it to the best of my abilities. I always find something to look forward to, in what I will call the "present future?" This future can be in the next hour or in the next part of my day. These are the times when I start to regain control over the attributes of the Dash as I have defined them above. This is when I start to think about how to make the present the best that I can make it. This thinking is not limited to controlling of Dash attributes; it can also be applied to the control of your resources. I try to do the same thinking about preserving and managing my resources. For instance, I turn the lights off in my home and I also turn them off in a hotel room when not needed. I love the hotel key systems that make you put your key in a switch to turn on the lights when you enter a room. Controlling time in the Dash framework is truly controlling a valuable resource.

As I am writing this chapter, I am in a very nice place, on an island listening to the surf, wind and birds. I am about to get on a boat to go to the mainland to go golfing. The scenery around me is beautiful. This is a tremendous time for me and my personal state of mind is experiencing total peace. My pace is what I would call a comfortable rhythm and I am in control. Meaning, I am the one dictating what happens to me next. Today, I know both I and God are in control and that gives me great peace of mind. These are the times when the speed of your Dash is close to perfect.

Since I am discussing controlling the speed of the Dash, I should also discuss how easy it is to lose control over the speed and what makes it go too fast or too slow. Usually, it is when I am dealing with other people in my life. These people could be colleagues, friends or family members, or various situations inside my Dash Club structure. I have to find the flow that works for me inside of my structure and sometimes inside of theirs. This is a time when I know I am not in total control and there can be times when I may have very little control over the circumstances. This is the time when you must work hard to keep the pace of your Dash from racing out of your control. You must understand what you can and can't control and seek comfort in that understanding. This is a time for you to think about that "present future," as I described earlier. We need to pick the pieces we can control. Don't get me wrong, there are times when my Dash spins out of my control more than I like. These are the times when I work the hardest to see what part of it I can control and I usually find many things I can control. I purport that there should never be a time when you have no control. An example of this discussion is presented through the character Ruben played by Denzel

Washington in the movie, "The Hurricane," (based on a true story). When he was falsely accused of murder, Ruben was very careful to not let people give him too much false hope or gain full control over the speed of his Dash. He knew he could do the time in jail, if he didn't lose too much control over the situation. He would not even surrender to hope at this time during his life. The quality of his Dash was at an all time low, but he was still controlling its speed. His Dash was being defined by being locked in a penal institution some twenty plus years for something he didn't do. For a long time he fought the system; he fought the demons in his head; he even fought his wife and sent her off to marry someone else. He knew if he was going to live inside this prison world, he could not let himself be too attached to the outside world. Reuben regained hope when a young man named Lazarus read the book he had written about his life in prison. Lazarus helps restore Reuben's hope by visiting him and by believing in his innocence. With help from Lazarus and the Canadians (people who helped Lazarus leave a life of poverty), Reuben not only regained control over his Dash, he worked for years until he regained his freedom. Each time I watch the movie it makes me rededicate my life to doing things right for me and for others. I am sure I don't fully comprehend what Reuben's life was like inside of all that mayhem and hate. What I do know is I have an opportunity to enjoy life to its fullest, if I work at each day as if it were my last.

Another example of losing control of the speed of your Dash happens to me often when working. At one company I worked for, my boss was a very aggressive man and he would call you at the drop of a hat and ask you to make something happen in some strange part of the world. When he called, you immediately lost control of the speed of your Dash. Fortunately, he would call several of us and usually one of us would get the situation under control in short order. I have learned when he is involved in the situation, you must listen to him carefully and then let him know you heard and understand every thing he has said to you. Usually, I would formulate a quick plan that I would share with him about how I was going to address the situation and ask if he thought this was a way to get started. He usually did not let you know he agreed with you at the first presentation of the solution, but he was very good at delegation and he knew he had several sources working on it, so he was willing to release it to you, immediately. Once I got his early by-in, I would formulate a more complete plan and go back to him and present the solution with more detail. This allowed me to gain back more control of the speed of my Dash in these situation. This was often a weekly encounter with this particular manager.

Again, I think the speed of your Dash is a subset of the quality of your Dash. If it is spinning out of control, the quality of your Dash is denigrated. When you regain control, you regain a very important parameter of the quality of your Dash back under your control. Yes, it is all about control.

Here is one final example of a spousal relationship and how easy you can lose control over the speed of your Dash. I was on a great vacation in Singapore and I was my usual planning self. I made all of the reservations for the plane and hotels well in advance, utilizing the web. The web is a great tool for accomplishing all of the reservation stuff, but it can lead you down a path that can deceive you. I found out from a colleague of mine that Beach Road would be a good area to stay in, when we are in Singapore. On the web I found that Beach Road runs through the heart of the city and has great hotels and restaurants on it. Being the great web surfer that we all have become, I googled for a hotel and found the perfect spot or so I thought. It was priced right, it had all the amenities I thought my wife and I might need and it was perfectly located. On the web, the pictures of the hotel looked great. I smiled and put my credit card to work. I got confirmation and went happily to bed.

When we arrived in Singapore full of excitement, we hopped in a taxi with our luggage and golf clubs in tow. We were taken to this lively corner that had a lot of vibrant activity with people still eating at 12:00 pm at night. We saw two gentlemen sitting outside, who we later found eager to take our luggage to our rooms. We went up a funky elevator to the second floor, where we immediately realized our Dash speed was out of control. First they said, they had no more rooms and I immediately whipped out my confirmation and the desk clerk realized he needed to honor it. He found a room and had the bell hop help us to it. We had to step over various things in the hall way that should have been stored away. When we got to the room, it had the odor of an ancient tomb mixed with cigarette smoke. My wife was livid and aimed it at me. "You found us this cheap hotel and it stinks," she said. I watched my Dash spin out of control as we both became angry and uncomfortable with the situation. We were jet lagged, hungry and tired. At the recommendation of one the bell hops, we went down to the corner and ate an interesting meal and then went promptly to bed. Well, the next two weeks of vacation were colored by this first experience. The control came back quickly when we arrived at the great resort I described earlier on a wonderful secluded island called Bantayan off the Coast of Cebu Island in the Philippines. Once I was on the golf course and looking at the ocean over the seventh green, my Dash flowed nicely again. Again, this discussion is truly about what you control and the situations you put yourself in. I will admit I let my attitude get a little funky when my wife didn't seem to understand it wasn't my fault. Yep, she is a very important part of my Dash structure in the club and affects the quality good and bad. Having chosen a great hotel in the next place we visited helped us regain control over the speed of our Dash. It required some work to reshape our attitudes and get back to having fun. One of the things my wife and I have going for us is we love to play golf and we always plan our vacations around beautiful golf course. Once we are on a golf course we are happy. You should find this kind of sanctuary for your Dash.

Conspiracy of the Urgent!

I have a golf buddy who is also a pastor of outreach at our church. His name is Tim Kauk and I want to acknowledge him for his contribution to this discussion. During one of his sermons, he presented an excellent message that was one of a series of messages. The series of messages was themed "Get a Life" with the by line of "God wants so much more for you than to merely exist." During the message he presented and discussed an interesting concept called "Conspiracy of the Urgent."

Tim's concept of the "Conspiracy of the Urgent," simply stated says, "first and foremost we create urgency for the sake of urgency. Everything in life to day has an undercurrent of urgency. We have become agents of the urgent. We don't have time for anything because we are too busy trying to do everything. This is another one of those concepts that shows how we are building "being out of control" into our society. It fits into this discussion of understanding and gaining control of the speed of your Dash and presents some things to think about.

For example, I have a friend that is a part of my Dash Club structure who realized that he was going to the cafeteria and grabbing what ever there was he could grab quickly to eat and eating it at his desk. He was doing this because he felt he didn't have time for lunch. He needed to work while he was eating his lunch. He realized he was eating bad food and working right through his lunch. The conspiracy was that he was creating the urgency to get more work done. He was not only sacrificing his health by eating poorly, he was also stressing himself out more because he was working non-stop through the day without a break. He then realized he was not using his benefit that afforded him a membership at the local gym because he had no time in the evening due to reading email after he grabbed a quick meal in the evening. He realized he was gaining a lot of weight and was getting out shape. He also realized the company was not appreciating all of this extra effort. In fact they took away some of his responsibility due to the business he was helping manage wasn't quite going the way they had envisioned. He became very frustrated and disenchanted with the company. He truly had lost control of the speed of his Dash.

Today, if you see him, he looks great! He has lost a lot of weight. When I call him to go to lunch he is usually headed out to the gym to work out. He still grabs a quick lunch on his way back to the office after his workout, but it is usually a healthier lunch than before. In my opinion he still works too hard, because he still works weekends and evenings, but he at least has slowed his Dash down enough to look and feel good again.

What is it about our society, today, that makes us so urgent in almost everything we do? We seem to have no time to do the things we really would like to do. This is a conspiracy we ought to put an end to. This is simply a matter of gaining control. Like my buddy, we need to realize what we are allowing ourselves to create these urgencies and then change the thinking and the behavior that brings them about. Yes, I know it is not as easy as I make it sound here in this book, but I have to encourage you to start somewhere. Conspiracy of the Urgent, are you one its agents? Thanks Tim!

The discussions above tell us how easy it is to allow our Dash to spin out of our control. In the end it is about what we allow to happen to us and take away our control over where we want our lives to go and how we want to participate in the club. I hope to continue to encourage you to look at your life with the intent to enjoy every minute of it and not to beat a "dead horse" all puns intended, to continue or start living your life to the fullest!

Chapter 1

Dash Actions:

1. Read this book with an open mind!
2. Learn from your mistakes and celebrate when you get something right!
3. Learn to value time, both yours and others!
4. Understand what you can and can't control!
5. Work to control and manage your time and resources to the best of your ability!
6. Help family, friends and colleagues to manage their time and resources when the opportunity presents itself!
7. Be aware of how you impact someone else's Dash!
8. Find a sanctuary for your Dash. It should be something you really like to do. Mine is golf!
9. Manage urgency to the best of your abilities!

Chapter 2

YOUR BIRTHDAY!

I wrote the chapter above knowing that I would get ahead of myself concerning how, chronologically, the sequence of events on the headstone happens. Remember on the headstone the Birthday, the Dash and then the Deathday is presented sequentially. I wanted the first chapter to be one of definition that would describe the Dash Club and then we could continue to look at how to build and take advantage of its structure. Now that we have defined the Dash Club, I need to back up and discuss the significance of your birthday in the Dash Club structure. We all know that the living of a life starts at birth, hence your "Birthday."

Your birthday is the first day of your life and it is the beginning of creating your Dash. It is amazing to think that after your tiring and tortuous journey down the birth canal, the first thing everyone wants you to do, the minute you get into this world, is cry. When that doctor holds you upside down by your feet and slaps you on your naked tender butt, you had better cry or everyone gets worried. It would be nice if this was the last time you cried, but not likely. Your cry is the first time you will communicate with the world and the people who love you and these people will likely continue to love you most of your life and/or most of their lives. From this day forward you will spend a significant amount of time learning the things you need to know and do to live the rest of your life.

Interestingly enough, this first time you cry kicks off a great and wonderful celebration of your entry into this world. All of the people who care about you are waiting in great anticipation for you to come and cry for them. Once you have cried, these people start hugging and enjoying each other long before they ever get to hug and enjoy you. Many of them cry with great joy once they know you have cried. For a long time to come you are dependent on some of these people to help you get your Dash off to a good start. Soon as you are done crying and they get you all cleaned up, they then want you to eat, drink and rest. This makes for a joyous and interesting day for everyone. You and many of the folks who were there at your birth will celebrate on this day for many years to come. This will be a day set aside to celebrate your existence for as long as you live. Your Birthday!

This day is also the first day of the rest of your life. Once you comprehend that each day you live is the first day of the rest of your life, you will start to approach life with great excitement and appreciation. You will not want to waste any of it. You will start to cherish life and attempt to enjoy every minute of it in every way you can! This does not happen overnight and for some of us it takes a long time to reach such a marvelous understanding of the value of life.

Now let's step back again and look at how the birth process begins. Let's look at it as a model for how we might accomplish many of the things that make our lives successful. First, there is the conception that may be started with a romantic evening that results in the ecstasy of a great and pleasurable moment between a man and woman who loves each other very much. The interesting thing here is that there is at least one very intensive moment that lasts a matter of seconds. It is in this moment that it all gets started. All pain and pleasure start out this way. They are usually very intense moments and hopefully, you experience these moments as feelings of pleasure and very few of them as experiences of pain. The orgasm is one example of pleasure and stubbing your toe is an example of pain. Throughout life you will deal with pleasures and pains and you will want to manage their intensity.

Next, there is a time of anticipation that leads up to getting the news that there has been a successful conception. This can be a time of uncertainty or anxiousness. This is a time where we may be tested as to how patient we can be. The ability to be patient is not to be taken lightly. I have found my lack of patience has led me to much of my emotional pain, if not to much of my physical pain. When I have employed patience, I and the people that surround me have often experienced great pleasure.

Then there is the moment in time where we find out we are successful in conceiving what we started out to do. What is most interesting about this part of the process or shall we call it the journey (which I will often use interchangeably with process); it is only the beginning. It is the beginning of the joy that will be weaved throughout some of the unpleasant feelings a woman might feel during her pregnancy. But, the hope is, the good will always out weigh the bad. Hopefully, we will forget the uncomfortable times and only remember the good times along the way.

Now comes another time of waiting. In the case of creating a life that culminates into a birth, it takes nine months for the journey to be completed. This is all froth with anticipation and excitement. Ladies, I do not want you to think I am ignoring all the things that can go wrong or the pain and suffering that is also a part of this journey. I am just attempting to set up a thinking process of how we can go through life with a positive perspective that is for sure to enhance the way we might choose to approach life even during the painful times. I think learning to minimize the process of handling emotional or physical pain will enhance our lives. Learning to maximize the joy goes with out saying. The journey has begun.

I have always believed if I can understand how to begin something, then I can understand how to enjoy the process and finally get the desired results I am looking to achieve. When it comes to living, we often forget how enjoyable it is to get things started. We forget how much we look forward to the birth of a child. I think we should approach a new idea or a fresh start with the same excitement and vigor. I would like to offer that we look at the birth process as a good model for helping you start whatever accomplishments you desire in life. The thing to remember is - this journey starts out very positive and your involvement is one of the main reasons why it is such a glorious beginning. We should anticipate the problems that might occur and again minimize the negatives for as long as you can celebrate the accomplishments.

After experiencing a great beginning such as the birth of a child, each and everyday should be a big deal no matter what is going on in our lives. If you are alive and well, then it should be an even bigger deal. I start each day thanking God for my life and the life of others that I love. I try not to stop with just my immediate family, but I give thanks for others who positively influence my life at various points in time.

If we look at this process as an approach for how most of the things we do in life are brought to fruition, we get an understanding of how we can better enjoy the process as much as we enjoy the successful results. In this case, we get an exceptional bundle of joy, a child. The conception of great ideas and thoughts are equally joyful to experience. Now we have life.

Chapter 2

Dash Actions:

1. Celebrate each day as if it is the last day of your life!
2. Take the initiative to start things as often as you can!
3. Learn to enjoy the process of creating something as much as you enjoy the results!
4. Minimize the negatives that come your way!
5. Dwell as long as you can on the positives!
6. Learn to enjoy the journey as much as you enjoy the beginning and the end!

Chapter 3

UNDERSTANDING HOW GOOD IT IS!

The "It" is life in America the beautiful! We often forget why our fore fathers and mothers started this country; it was and still is to enjoy life to its fullest with freedom and hope as its standard fare.

By now, you have realized I am an eternal optimist, yet I know that all of our experiences are not always positive. Many people eat wrong, don't exercise, lack education for living life, refuse to obey the law, create bad relationships, have the wrong friends, don't have a great spiritual life, are in too much debt, do not make good investments with their time or their money, work at jobs they hate and spend way too much time complaining about it all. I believe this is all due to not thinking correctly and making bad choices. I guarantee you one thing I know about these people I just described, their lives are miserable and they just want to see the day come to its end.

I assure you, they haven't taken the time to realize all that they have. They should be ashamed of themselves, because they are missing a great and wonderful life. I personally don't know many of these people, because many of them are not a part of my Dash Club structure. When I am around these types of people, I am usually trying to convince them to think differently. As a Dash Club Evangelist and I hope you will become one after reading this book, I believe my mission in life is to make this world a better place, when and wherever I can. Living here in America presents me with a lot of opportunities to do just that. I have come to understand that opportunity doesn't mean entitlement. It means, if you can grab the brass ring you can keep it!

The majority of our experiences should be wonderful and exciting. If our lives are not what we think they ought to be, we should be reassessing our goals and strategies and figuring out how to change our lives. I am of the belief that we are what we make ourselves to be. Even in tragedy there is a silver lining and you can get inside of it, if you wish to make your life better. Sometimes finding that lining is not easy, but it is always there. I thought Christopher Reeves modeled this behavior marvelously after his horse riding accident. When I think of how he believed that he would walk again and how that belief not only gave him hope, but gave hope to all who encountered him, especially his wife, family and friends. He truly inspired many people and that includes me.

Remember, this was the guy we knew as Superman, one of our childhood heroes. Before his accident, he embodied good looks, fame and fortune. He appeared to be married to a good woman and his children seemed happy. In this land, we would call him successful. When tragedy befell him and his family, he learned to approach the journey of getting back to health with great positiveness. I remember seeing him on a Barbara Walter's TV Special and hearing him explain to us what it was like to get off the respirator just for a second or two, to afford him the chance to smell a rose again. Again, this was inspirational to all of us. He showed us we can never give up on living. Having this kind of tragedy befall you in many other countries would leave you for a dreaded and miserable existence. In America he was able to embrace the tragedy and make it a life worth living. He had the opportunity to gain the finances, fame and technology to go forth. He used it all to create great experiences for his family and for himself.

On a more personal level, I have a life-long friend that I have known for many years. He gave up a very lucrative career as an aircraft mechanic in the Boeing Company to answer a call to the ministry and has devoted his life to helping others realize their spiritual potential. This friend does not have a lot of money, but does have a great family consisting of four children and a wife. I see this friend about every two to three years and usually try to spend some quality time with him and his wife as often as our schedules and finances permit.

Once, I invited him and his wife to come spend some time with us on the coast of Southern California. I knew he couldn't afford to spend time socializing in expensive places like Laguna Beach or Balboa Island or Newport Beach without some financial assistance from me and my family. We worked out a deal for him and his wife to fly down for a four day weekend. My goal was to give them some down time and great experiences that would last a lifetime for both them and us. By the way, I did this as much for me and my wife, as I did it for them. (In a later chapter I will discuss why doing some things for selfish reasons is good for your Dash.)

We took them to a lavish brunch at a bistro on Newport Beach. We took them for walks around Balboa Island. We spent some time eating at a fabulous restaurant in Laguna Beach while watching a spectacular sunset over the ocean. We finally drove up the coast to eat at our favorite restaurant in the beautiful Pacific Palisades. Each activity was a great experience and created memories to treasure for the rest of our lives. By the time the weekend was over, we didn't want to see it end and it made for spending some great times together with some very caring and adoring friends. When we parted, we all realized it was all about sharing time together and enjoying some great experiences together. As my buddy got on his plane, he looked back and smiled at me and said, "I will see you soon Doc!" It was as if, he would be back in a week! Even as I write this, I get all warm and fuzzy inside and just want to remember that pleasant smile and those wonderful times we shared with one another. Life truly is about great experiences and good memories.

Another memorable time was a vacation shared by me and my wife. We had the wonderful pleasure of visiting the Hawaiian Islands. I can still remember the smell of the freshly harvested pineapple as we rode horses in the pineapple fields on Maui. I can smell the pineapple even now when I close my eyes and let my mind wonder back to that great memory. This is an experience that I can relive again and again. Seeing the excitement on my wife's face and hearing the gentle snorting of the horse, as it gently pranced through the dirt and through the pineapple stalks was worth it all. Reliving this experience as often as I can makes for a great enhancement to my Dash.

Now, let me be perfectly clear, if you don't have the means to take great and exciting vacations abroad, you can still make great memories spending quality time with friends and family right here at home. (I will discuss more on creating a good support system with your friends and family members in a later chapter. I will also discuss achieving workable finances in another chapter.) Living in the United States of America affords us many places and things to see and experience. If you throw in all the different cultures represented by all the different people here in the US, you can have some great times.

In this great land, the different ethnicities make for fabulous social experiences. Just imagine the representation; we have people of African decent, Asian decent, European decent and the richness of the Spanish influence, the German influence, the Japanese influence to name a few. Living in Arizona affords me the vast richness of the Native American cultural influences on my life. There is little doubt that America is a melting pot. The pot is full and rich when it comes to ethnic cultures that represent the world.

I don't know about you, but these cultures influence my Friday night dinner plans on a regular basis. Here is part of a conversation I have been known to have with my wife on some Friday nights, "Well dear, what do you feel like eating tonight, will it be Chinese, Vietnamese, Mexican or Italian?" These are just some of the choices I will put in front of her. Guess what, she is Filipino and on any given night we will have the taste of the Philippines with foods such as lumpia, pancit or chicken adobo right at home. My friends love to come over and enjoy good dining.

These cultures influence the music I listen to. I grew up listening to what we called, Soul Music. But in this day and age, I have come to truly appreciate a jazzy Spanish guitar solo as played by Marc Antoine. Or a wonderful up tempo alto sax as played by Jeff Kashiwa. Or enjoy the soulful, contemporary, gospel sung by Karen Grant. Carlos Santana still thrills me at every listen. I truly enjoy the European flavor that Sting brings to music and I thoroughly enjoy Eric Clapton and the piano sensation - Alicia Keyes. I am equally comfortable listening to Irish music as presented by Michael Flatley and company. I love the incredible chill I get listening to Asian themes on instruments that I cannot even pronounce their names. Once, I heard a band from China playing Take 5 in a way I never heard it played before.

The American culture has finally embraced the influence that Black people have had on music. You cannot watch an action movie without the driving drum and punching lyrics of rap as the main feature in the sound track. It is now a plus to have a rapper associated with the production of the film and rappers turned actors are creating a new genre of movies that are still a bit exploitive of the Black culture, but assimilation of this music into the American culture is now occurring.

Another example of this cultural phenomenon is the assimilation of the Vietnamese People into the American culture. Many years ago I went home to visit New Orleans and my dad took me to buy some boiled crawfish. Before I left home to see the world most of the seafood stores were not in our local neighborhoods. They were in other parts of town mostly occupied by White Americans, such as Johnny's Seafood Market or Shirley's Seafood Place. On this occasion, my dad drove just a short distance from the house, where I spent most of my teenage years. We stopped at what looked to be a converted garage with a bunch of large covered tubs. We got out of the car and started to look under the covers and there were all types and assortments of seafood on ice. There were succulent crabs, large gulf shrimp and of course sacks of Louisiana boiled crawfish. If you haven't tasted some of these edible jewels of the sea, you haven't lived yet. The people selling this seafood were Vietnamese people still looking as if they had just got off the refugee boats. But here is the kicker; I went back to visit New Orleans a few years later and that garage looking shop was gone. Down under the big new freeway was a nice, big, new Seafood Store called Huynh's Seafood. The guy behind the counter was wearing Dockers and speaking the English of Bill Clinton and George Bush with a Vietnamese accent. What a country we live in!

A few years back I moved to sunny, Orange County in California for four years and what absolutely, overwhelmingly, surprised me was a drive up I-405 through the Santa Ana/Costa Mesa area. There was a sign on the freeway that said, "Little Saigon." Being the inquisitive, explorer and nosey sort that I am, I pulled off to see this place called Little Saigon. To be honest, what I expected to see were some bungalows and thatch roof houses with little runny nose kids running around with no shoes on, begging for nickels. Like the poverty I saw when I visited that part of the world. But, in Little Saigon there were only signs of prosperity and what I saw was even more surprising. It was a whole little city of big shops, markets and offices in major thriving business complexes sprawling for miles in every direction. There were major large super markets full of Asian foods and goods with in blocks of each other. There were doctors and dentist's offices, realtors, jewelry shops and of course lots of restaurants. The place was thriving with Vietnamese people conducting good ole American commerce. They were buying everything in sight and driving the nicest cars, mostly Mercedes, BMWs and Hondas. There were Vietnamese behind the counters selling the goods and all kinds of different people in front of the counters buying the goods. My wife and I bought some seafood and it was absolutely fresh and great. If you think that is great, let's explore how the people indigenous to this land are fairing: The Native American People.

If you are my age you probably are still using the politically incorrect term of Indians. Yes, they are a thriving part of America although slow in population growth. Never-the-less, they have discovered education in the law, engineering, business gaming, political science, as well as other disciplines. They now use government policies and old treaties to their advantage. They have found a niche in the gambling industry and in the name of tribal affairs are starting to compile some serious cash in those new tribal specific branches of their banks. Then there are the true Indians.

The other people we call Indians (from India) are faring nicely in America as well. They are the owners of most of the new software houses that are showing up all over the Silicon Valley. They are also the ones who own the venture capital firms that are backing and starting those firms. They don't need a sign saying little India. They are becoming so pervasive in the hi-tech world they would need many signs in many places. And as for the Persians who have found this great land, they to are enjoying a great life here in the land of opportunity.

It appears many of the ARCO gas station/corner groceries in Orange County are now owned by Persians. As a kid, I thought Persians sold and flew magic carpets in the movies. As an adult I have found, they own many of the carpet and rug stores and fly around the world on Lear Jets. In America, we don't even think of a rug with out thinking of a Persian rug. They live great lives in this country.

I could go on and on with many examples and you would agree that America is a good place for all kinds of people to live and make things happen. We live in the most thriving part of the world and we should never forget that it is a privilege. The people I have written about above truly understand and appreciate this idea of privilege.

Chapter 3

Dash Actions:

1. Become a Dash Club Evangelist!
2. You must have some great experiences in order to create and collect wonderful memories!
3. Sow positive seeds to all that you can!
4. Be open to change!
5. Inspire others when ever you can!
6. Live to enjoy people from all walks of life!
7. Respect and adore others as much as you would want them to respect and adore you!

Chapter 4

DO!

This is not a request; this is an order by me and Yoda to you. In the movie Star Wars the character Yoda tells Luke Skywalker, "don't try, you must do!" By what ever authority you allow me to have while you are reading this book, I want to encourage you to "do" the same. I have found that if you are really living, you are really doing, hence, the title of this chapter.

I would like to share a thought that came to mind one evening when I was writing checks to my creditors. As I was writing the checks, I realized that there was no more money left in my checking account. Yet, there were still more bills to be paid lying on the table. I ask you to take off your grammatical hat for a paragraph or two to fully appreciate this thought:

FOR ALL WHO MUST DO!

Do what you can with what you got!
Until you can get what you can get!
Or, until you can get what you need!
Or, until you can get what you WANT!

I now live by these words, and they have helped me control the desperation that would set in when I became overwhelmed by my lack of ability to control certain situations and/or circumstances, such as not being able to pay my bills. You too will have situations that are within your power to control, but you have not yet learned to control them. Now, if you can reach down and pull up all those things you haven't yet accomplished or even failed at making happen, which continues to frustrate you; you may realize they were not all that important in the first place. Or, maybe it is time to try them again! Or maybe it's time to forget them and start all over. Or just keep forging ahead and breaking totally new ground. Then remember this, "Do What You Can!

A Brief discussion: Maslow's Hierarchy of Needs

A small digression to discuss a topic that will help setup the thinking process for reading this book and giving you the proper perspective for receiving the information shared in this book.

During my freshman year in college, most students took a Psychology 101 class and we studied Maslow's Hierarchy of Needs. Its premise is based on a triangle that has different levels that represent a hierarchy. At the bottom level of the triangle are the basic things that people need to live their lives. These basic needs are: "Food, Water and Shelter, etc." At the top of the triangle is something called "Self Actualization." This is a level in life where we know who we are, we are at a station in life where we want to be and we have most of the things we need. This is where the good part of life starts and now we are able to focus on what we want. Some students of Maslow might debate me and say self actualization is when we have all we need and want. I think it is much more of a journey and not a finite process. If you are not totally familiar with this concept find a book and read up on this topic, I am sure you will find it interesting. Now with this framework in mind we can proceed with this discussion of "Do!" Now let's assess what you have already.

What You Got!

A good place to start is to figure out "what you got!" The question is what do you have? In other words let's take a survey of what we have in our bag already. In the last 200 years we now have the right to speak freely. We have the right to worship openly and as often as we like. We can buy a house or car. We can get married and have children. We can live, learn and become educated. We can stay healthy for many years. We have mostly what it takes to live a great and wonderful life. We now need to simply keep educating ourselves.

Education is a key component in the formula of success that leads to the great achievements we make happen in America. I believe the ability to gain the right information for living is indeed the pot of gold at the end of the rainbow. We are now able to receive education in every neighborhood and in almost any area of study we choose. I am aware that we still have work to do to bring about more social and economic equality for all Americans, but we are well on our way to making life good for all Americans. If education is the great equalizer we are making it possible for everyone that wants it.

Our politics is a very open process, although it is still dominated by wealthy people and mainly men. In the last twenty years we have had participation by more and more ethnic stake holders. Women are finding their stride through the education process and continue to gain ground in the business world. The senate is still male dominated, but the door is cracked open for her.

Our security was tested by 911 incidents, but it did not fail us. It has given us a reason to retrench and rethink who our international friends are and to be more careful with our resources. I believe we thought we were safer than the rest of the world and now we have become as safe as the rest of world. Being one who has traveled all over the world, our borders were not quite as safe as the rest of the world before 911. I think we have swung the pendulum to the other side and are making our gates quite hard to enter. We now understand the cost of safety and are willing to pay and put forth the effort to truly be safe.

I have a wonderful home in Arizona with a good wife and two good children. My children, because they still make some choices that lead them to struggles, have not quite learned to live the good life. Now that they are both in their twenties, I have a watchful eye on the choices they are making and will work hard to not interfere unless absolutely necessary. The good news is they are not married with children or in any great trouble with any one. They both seem to be trying to find themselves. I think many of you know what I mean. My house is a lovely place with great amenities that support our needs. For instance, we have five bedrooms, we have a four-hole putting green in half the yard and a hot tub and swimming pool in the other half. We live in a very nice middle class neighborhood. Crime is extremely low. This all leads to making life quite nice. We have plenty of room to entertain our friends and try to do that as often as we can. There is plenty of room to have family members come and stay during holidays. "This is what I got!" Take a minute and make your personal assessment! Now think about what you are able to get.

Until You Get What You Can Get!

I realized a long time ago that I wasn't going to get all the things I needed or wanted. I have a lot of things on my list that I want to accomplish before I die. For instance, I wanted four children, but my wife didn't want but two. I am glad I lost that argument, I am happy with the two. I wanted to be a famous musician. Now, I enjoy playing my horns in the church band. I have learned that I can grab some of the low hanging fruit at will. I have come to a great realization that I am capable of getting and accomplishing a lot of things. Sometimes I think we set our sights so high we make it too hard to get any thing. Sometimes I think we set our sights too low, we don't try to get very much! If you find it too hard to accomplish many things, you may not have your sights set at the right level for you. Again, ask yourself the question, what am I capable of getting?

Answering this question will help reprioritize what you set out to accomplish. Many of the good things that have come my way, I have had to work very hard to get. Other things have taken minimal effort. Getting some of those things has motivated me to accomplish many of my goals. An example of this is when you realize the investment you made in buying your home has paid off. You refinance your home and take cash out to pay off your other high interest debt. First, you get the satisfaction of lowering your stress from all the bills you have on your plate. Now you realize how good it feels to have money left over after you pay your bills. You are able to go out to dinner and not get anxious when they bring the bill to the table. This is a real freeing experience, to know you can pay your way. You are not trying to buy all those expensive toys you have on the list. You are simply getting the things you know you can afford. "This is truly getting what you can get and not necessarily what you need!"

Until You Get What You Need!

What do you really need? This is a question that most of us don't have to ponder over and over to answer. I caution you to understand this question before attempting to answer it. I have finally come to grips with this overwhelming question, which, by the way, most of us will answer in a very materialistic manner! First and foremost there is very little you actually need in life. As we presented above in the discussion of Maslow, you need food, water, shelter and a toilet. Most of the things you think you need, when you search your heart you will find that you really don't need them as much as you may want to have them. In today's world, there are a few things that you really need to live a good life. You need good health and a sound mind. You need good relationships with family, friends and colleagues. You need an income! You need the income because to enjoy this wonderful life in America you need money. You need money to pay for the things America affords you. An income allows you get the things you need to take care of you and your family. If you work hard and smart in America you will have most of the things you need. I believe there is one other thing that you need. You need something to believe in when all else fails. I fill this need with God. I do not wish to force any of my beliefs on you, but I am giving you my perspective on living a full life. After you have what you need, everything else will be the things that you want. "When we realize how little we need, we then realize how much we really want!" Wanting is natural!

Until You Get What You Want!

In the Maslow discussion we discuss what happens after you meet all of your needs and what it means to reach a state of self-actualization. This is when you know who you are and where you are and what you are and what you truly need. Now you are able to go beyond the need to the want. So the question becomes, what do you want?

Answering this question for me the first time resulted in a list of ten things. Compare your list to my list below:

1. *An education*
2. *A great career*
3. *A wonderful wife*
4. *A girl child*
5. *A boy child*
6. *A fabulous home*
7. *God in my life*
8. *A XJ6 Jaguar*
9. *A motor home*
10. *Investments*

I think this was a great list for a young 24 year old and believe it or not, this list hung on my refrigerator for over ten years. I remember one day I looked on the list and realized I was crossing off the last thing. Yes, I was about 34 four years young. I was happy, I had accomplished everything on my list, but I realized one thing, I was not done and life was not over. Today, if I were to construct this list of "wants" with the knowledge I have gained over the years, I would put "learn to live life one day at a time," at the top of the list, in the middle of the list and at the bottom of the list. I think the table of contents of this book gives you a good idea of what my list looks like today.

Chapter 4

Dash Actions:

1. Be a doer and not a whiner!
2. Be willing to give and you will often receive (get)!
3. Know what you can get and control!
4. Pay attention to your needs first and then your wants!
5. Don't want what you know you can't get!
6. Set realistic goals for yourself. Don't be afraid to write them down and display them for your regular viewing!
7. Work hard for what you want and you will get it!

Chapter 5

THE DASH THINKING PROCESS!

Cognitive Dissonance is the ability to have your thinking process be at odds with your ability to meet your desires in reality. Your mind will work hard to get rid of the dissonance and bring your thinking in line with reality. One example of this is when you go to a car dealership to buy a car. You want a blue car, but the salesperson says that they don't have a blue car at this time, but they can get one for you by next week. You want the car today and you are refusing to wait for the car you think you want later. You ask the salesperson to show you the same car in other colors. You now see the same car, but it is red. The salesperson explains that there is nothing different about the two cars except for their color. They both have leather interior, bucket seats, a Bose sound system and good gas mileage. You walk around the showroom and look at the cars that are there and you start to get comfortable with the beauty of the cars. You see a beautiful gray car and you slowly start to like it. After walking around the car a few more times, you fall in love with it. You finally turn to the salesman and you tell him you want this one - the gray one.

You stare at the gray one and you become more and more infatuated with having it. You tell him you like the gray one even more than you would have liked the blue one. He smiles and says to you, "good!" You have just experienced cognitive dissonance – having your thinking at odds with reality. But you don't allow the dissonance to stay around long. You will create the perceptions you need to make the realities you want.

Most of this book focuses on encouraging you to make your life as good as it can be and half of enjoying life is the perceptions of what is going on around you. If you perceive things are good it is very likely that things are good. The old adage that perception often becomes reality is very true. If I get up on Monday and allow myself to think, this is Blue Monday and the weekend is over and I got the blahs. I will treat the day like I perceive it, to be gloomy and I will likely be less productive. And my whole day will be something I simply want to see end. I will have wasted a significant portion of my life, one whole day. If I train myself that Mondays are blue I will waste a very large portion of my life trying to get to Tuesday. This type of thinking is devastating and should not be allowed. If I think that Friday is the end of the week and I should be tired. Every Friday I will find my self tired and all I will want to do is get Friday over so I can go home and be tired. I will waste another significant part of my life. I would much rather think, wow it is Monday and it is the first day of the new week. I can take this thinking forward and Monday becomes a day I will look forward to experiencing each and every week. If I look at Friday as day that concludes a productive week and it will be rewarded with the completion of my task list. I will then look forward to taking my wife out to dinner and coming home and enjoying the movie I bought from the video store on my way home. How exciting your life becomes with this level of productive thinking.

In fact, I highly recommend, that we should have something to look forward to in every day and let our minds wrap around it whenever it needs motivation. It is like telling a kid they are going to get ice cream if they eat their green beans. They will endure the beans until they get to the opportunity of enjoying the process of getting and eating ice cream. Having an event or process that you can look forward to in your day makes that day an exciting experience.

I present this type of thinking process to be used as the foundation for the rest of this discussion on being a member in the Dash Club. Getting our thinking in a state of clearness and profoundness will help us enjoy our lives. This is the ultimate thing in life that will lead to you having control over most of your Dash.

When I realized that to think clearly is to live a unique and awesome life, I think as often as I can. I love to just enjoy thinking about the future and its possibilities. Even when you are not in control, your thinking will help you manage well. I have gotten so intrigued with the ability to think clearly, I will not eat, drink, pour, shoot or introduce nothing into my body that will alter my thinking. I do not let any substance whatsoever alter my thought process. This is one of the greatest enhancements to my Dash that I can share with you.

The techniques are simple:
1. Put nothing in your body that will negatively alter your state of being or mind.
2. Find places that the minute you enter them you are automatically put in a state of peace and calm.
3. Clear your mind of all negative thoughts first, let them happen and move them out of your way.
4. Decide and control what you want to think about and do not accept negative thoughts from your self or no one else.
5. Work at the process for enjoyment and don't let the

process become work even though you might be in the act of working.

Here is an example of executing the above process. Sometimes on my way to work I turn off all music and other outside influences and start to calm myself. I put a smile on my face and I look for pretty plants or trees along the way. I like the desert of Arizona and I find beauty in cacti, good landscaping and well manicured bushes, colors of buildings that stand out. If I am on my way to work, I will think about what is ahead in my day and I have already discussed how we need to find things in our day to look forward to. If I am leaving work I will think about what great thing I am going to do to relax when I get home. Often I find my self solving problems that I couldn't solve just a few hours earlier.

If you get a chance to be some where special as I will share below in Dash memories and have the opportunity to do clear thinking, you will truly experience the ultimate action of control. I highly recommend that you create sanctuaries where you can go and do uninterrupted clear thinking. There are people who don't have a clue about having the ability to control their thinking and make thinking an exciting process to enhance their lives. Hey, you don't have to solve problems or do work; sometimes you can just have neat, fun thoughts. This type of thinking can become recreational; you can create some great Dash memories along the way that you will use to enhance this process.

Dash Memories

Making memories is one of my favorite things to do. I've always thought if I were flat on my back, I would pray that I still have my ability to think and to go back into my memory banks and grab some of the great memories I have made in life. Your memories may be more valuable than money when you get towards the end of the Dash and you can't do the things you use to do. I am sure this was what made Christopher Reeves, his wife and kids have such great hope during the last part of finalizing his Dash. I already have things I don't do any more but, I love to remember doing them. I can remember the smiles on my children's faces the first time they saw Mickey at Disneyland. I have many great memories of camping and hiking with my kids.

I use to love to ski with my children and my wife. We lived in Seattle and Oregon one of the best places in the United States for skiing. I started skiing on a dare from a crazy friend that taunted me while I was in the Navy. He would to say to me, you people from the south can't ski. I must admit that motivated me beyond belief to show him that I could. At the time, I didn't pay attention to his accent, which I came to realize was from Texas. Yes, he was from the south. The first time I hit the slopes with this person taunting me, I got right up on my skis, felt the exhilaration and was hooked. I skied on the mountains of Canada, Washington and Oregon. I don't ski much these days, but I love to remember the times I did. Today skiing has been replaced by playing a lot of golf down here in Arizona.

I truly enjoyed sailing the seven seas as a Navy seaman. I remember meeting and working with great people. It was the first time I heard more people speaking a different language than my own. I often think back to being in Australia and meeting several beautiful women that I could have married. I shared earlier that I married a beautiful Filipino woman that I met while being home ported in Subic Bay Philippines. Yes, I am still married to her after 28 years at the writing of this book.

I shared earlier about horse back riding through a pineapple field in Maui with my wife. It is worth mentioning again. This was truly an extraordinary experience that I feel everyone should have at least once in their lives. I have some great childhood memories.

I still remember being a bunny in my kindergarten class in elementary school. I remember my teacher Mrs. Harrington herding all of us little five year old bunnies on to the stage and we performed the bunny hop dance. What a kick to be able to go back and enjoy such an intimate experience. The childhood experiences are the ones that will stick with us for the longest and will be treasured by most of us.

These great experiences lead to some great memories for future enjoyment. I understand that we have many experiences that we don't want to remember. I don't know about you, but I simply don't remember most of them and I cling to those valued treasured memories. I think you should make so many positive memories that they will overwhelm the thought of a negative one. Making these memories will happen as a by product, if you lead and live a wonderful life.

It is very important to share your life and allow others to help make and share your memories. There is nothing better than the memories you make and share with others. I think people were made for other people. Yes, you must take care of yourself first, but you must also be willing to share and take care of others. The best thinking I ever do is reliving great memories and that is what Dash thinking is all about.

Chapter 5

Dash Actions:

1. Think clearly and often!
2. Create a maintainable reality for yourself!
3. Don't waste precious time, you can't get it back!
4. Know that positive thinking is not over rated, but it is underutilized!
5. Create great memories; you will need them later in life!
6. Put nothing in your body that will negatively alter your state of being or mind!
7. Find places that the minute you enter them you are automatically put in a state of peace and calm!
8. Make it a practice to clear your mind of all negative thoughts quickly!
9. Decide and control what you want to think about and do not accept negative thoughts from yourself or no one else!
10. Work at the process for enjoyment and don't let the process become work even though you might be in the act of working!

Chapter 6

ON SELF!

Many people believe that putting too much focus on ones self is a poor character trait and there are people who project a negative portrayal of selfishness. They actually appear to not care about anyone except themselves, hence their selfishness.

I would like to explore another take on being selfish or should I say more on "a healthy focus on self" and how it could help enhance the Dash Club structure. I have often been told that I am selfish or I pay too much attention to myself; of course this is told to me by my wife and kids. Many times they do it in jest, but I keep a running joke with them about how it helps them as much as it helps me when I am meeting the desires for myself. If truth were to be told, they are often telling me what they have observed or experienced when dealing with me. What makes them do this? If I bought something to eat that I really like to eat, like a pint of fruit sorbet, I would buy two and label one for me and one for them. I did this because I would buy it and save it for a time when I wanted it. Those times when I really wanted it, it would be gone. In their eyes this is considered a selfish act. They see it as me not wanting to share my pint with them. It is true we often make decisions that are for our personal enjoyment and gain, but we shouldn't let it adversely or negatively affect our family members and friends. I truly love people, but it is clear that I love me and my life more and it is my guess you do too, if you have a normal healthy ego.

Self preservation is the first law of nature and we all subscribe in some manner. In this discussion, when I talk about self, I am talking about taking care of yourself to the best of your abilities and with all the resources you can bring to the table for this purpose. I am talking about giving you every chance to be successful, healthy, wealthy, wise and happy. As I have often stated, you had better learn to take good care of your self before trying to take care of someone else.

Yes, I am a subscriber to the method of putting on your oxygen, before you attempt to put the oxygen on someone else. On the surface this is appears to be a selfish act. But, consider the consequences of trying to put on someone else's oxygen, before you have secured your own breathing. Not only might you lose them due to your lack of oxygen, but you also risk losing you and that would be tragic for both. This analogy is one that should be thought through many times in our endeavor to being a member in good standing in the Dash Club.

I have made many decisions that were motivated by me that produced positive results for me and many times over for my family, friends and other people. The funny thing about many of these decisions, they are often the basis for most of my personal enjoyment and for my family, friends and others to enjoy right along with me. I believe my family and friends have benefited much from my, so called, "self-centered decisions." I have ventured into to all kinds of fun experiences trying to enjoy myself and my family and friends have enjoyed the benefits of those ventures right along with me.

For example, I play the saxophone and I use to tell my mother that I did not want to see my girlfriend until I was done with my practice sessions. If my girlfriend came over during my sessions, she got to spend some quality time with my mother. It was very gratifying to learn to play the sax and to be in a marching band that participated in the New Orleans, Mardi Gras activities. It is even more gratifying to play in the church's worship band and know that one to two thousand people will have the opportunity to enjoy listening to me play for them. This is a powerful experience each and every time it happens.

Once, my pleasing of self led me to the crazy notion of wanting to be a clown. (Some people might call it satisfying my curiosity.) I studied for many weeks and had a cool clown outfit. I did that for me and now several times a year I clown at church harvest festivals, daycares and several other neighborhood events. It is a most rewarding experience to make five year old twin girls smile at the same time. Can you imagine the memory I have of that? Another time I got all excited about puppeteering. I talked my family into helping make the puppets. All of my family got involved. In the end my daughter and I had many hours of enjoyment putting on puppet shows for kids. It is great enjoyment to see the smiling face of a kid due to something you are doing. I love to have people bring their kids over and allow me to show off my puppets to them. The kids love to touch the puppets and try to make them work.

One of my selfish ventures led me to owning a motor home. When my wife first heard of the idea, she thought I was just being foolish and spending money unnecessarily. Today, my wife would agree that motor home gave me and my family years of fun filled weekends on the Oregon Coast and we spent many great vacations running up and down the California beaches in great comfort. We have a treasure chest of memorable times together.

As you read earlier, I fulfilled my personal dream of owning a Jaguar and my daughter has years of fond memories riding in that Jaguar. She was often heard saying that I didn't look right in any other car, until I bought the G-35 by Infiniti. It is nice to have a daughter who wants the best for her father. Or is it the best for herself? Hmmm!

I have never shied away from my doing things I love to do, in fact, I try to embrace it and never let it get in the way of my relationships with other people. I usually include other people. I believe if you talk to the friends of my younger years, they might say, "Yes, Darrell was all about Darrell. He did everything he wanted to do." I believe if you talk to my friends of today, they would say, "he really embraces life and doesn't hold back and tries to enjoy every minute of it. He works hard to enjoy his life and he tries to help everyone enjoy life." I think I have learned to get rid of the negative implementations that make it appear that I am doing things for me only. I still like to take on new challenges that please me, but I thoroughly enjoy doing things for other people.

In a previous book, I dealt with this topic from a slightly different angle, "I wrote about the ego and where it fits. "I think the ego is about motivating yourself and letting that drive you to accomplish those things that really make you live life the best way you can. I think you need to be self-motivated and driven to accomplish your goals. Fortune magazine says the best executives of our time are arrogant, egotistical and often self-centered. But, along with those attributes that have led to their success come great leadership ability, good communication skills, great management skills and good motivational skills. They know how to inspire people. They know how to create camaraderie and build great teams. Whenever you hear some one like Jack Welch (GE) or Lou Gertzner (IBM) or Rick Warren (Purpose Driven Life) speak, you want to listen and you hang on to their every word. Their boldness excites you. They are mere men, but they live life, large and they have well polished skills, self-worth and an ego under control.

It takes great confidence in oneself to go for your dreams and in my opinion, this confidence is also a state of taking good care of yourself. You must really care enough about you to be able to make you happy. Most winners truly understand this state of mind. Most successful people first find success in being comfortable in their own skin. They understand that they must take care of themselves first. They are driven to improve themselves no matter what they are doing. Tiger Woods wins because that is what he has come to do. He has been known to say, "I was inside my self and I don't remember what is going on around me, I focus on what I am doing now." Earl Woods once shared with me, that he trained Tiger to focus on what he is doing at that moment and nothing else. Now, we all know Tiger can be distracted by the shutter of a camera or some other distraction in the crowd, but for the most part, he adapts to the surroundings and makes extraordinary things happen on a golf course. He is highly motivated and to watch him is captivating. Tiger Woods says, "I play golf to win and to come in second place is not an option." Is he highly motivated or is he being self-centered? In my opinion he uses positive self motivation and determination to win.

As I have shared earlier, this is my fourth book and I still haven't put one on the best sellers list, but I am as focused on making that happen as I was when I was writing the first one and I am convinced that this is the one. This is what I call a winning attitude based on a positive self-focus.

Winning in life is the ultimate feeling and it is how life

should be lived everyday. Once you get such an attitude, you become an unbeatable winner in life. I have found that people who acquire this approach to one's self and one's life, are the truly happy people and are great people to be around and they help make this world a better place for all of us.

A final thought on this positive focus on self, the ability to take care of one's self in health, wealth, spiritually and to help others while you are doing it makes for a great Dash attribute.

Chapter 6

Dash Actions:

1. Create a great self-image!
2. Know your self-worth!
3. Learn to motivate yourself first and then motivate others!
4. Take good care of your health, wealth, spiritual being and all the things that make for a great life!
5. Be positively focused on your self, first!
6. Never let what you are doing for your self negatively affect others!

Chapter 7

PEOPLE!

I wrote this book to encourage people to enjoy their lives. Hopefully, in the earlier chapters of this book I have been running a theme on life that is being lived by people for other people. I have found there are so many things that are done for the sake of doing them and not for their true intention. I love people! I absolutely live for people and I want people to live for me. I know I could not live on this earth with out other people. The thought of spending my life with out my wife, children and friends truly sends cold chills up my spine. I am at my best when I am around other people. What makes me get up in the morning is knowing I will be dealing with people.

In my travels around the world I have had the opportunity to experience people from many different cultures, worlds and walks of life. I have laughed out loud with a German business colleague. I have dined on succulent duck with my colleagues from China. I have sung karaoke with coworkers and customers in Korea. I have had debates with people in London. I have driven through Bavaria with colleagues from Singapore. I have had candlelight dinners with colleagues on a boat in Switzerland. I cherish every moment I have spent getting to know the people of these different worlds.

What is most interesting to me about people is that we are all very different in many ways and we are all alike in many ways. I have come to the conclusion that we all seek one major way to

Darrell D. Simms

be alike, we all desire a great long and prosperous life and we will do all we can to achieve that life. We may define what makes life "great," differently and with varying degrees, but we still seek it all the same.

   This act of seeking it is what gives us some common goals and choices to enjoy one another. For example, in China the people love to eat great food. In Africa they love to eat great food. In the Peru they love to eat great food and in Cuba they love to eat great food. If you allow these people to all visit each others lands, they won't agree on what foods are great. They will all agree that the act of sitting down together and eating the food is a wonderful way to spend some time together. Another thing people from all over the world agree on is sightseeing. In each country there are many beautiful places to visit and see. I think people from anyone of those places mentioned above would agree that "The Great Wall" in China is as much a wonder of the world as "The Grand Canyon" in America or the mountains in Switzerland or the waterfalls in Italy. They might not all agree that seeing a lake as a result of a dam being built is a great thing to see.

   I personally have learned to enjoy life through other people and one person that has taught me well is my wife. She is of another culture that is very different from mine. I have learned to enjoy life through her eyes and from her experiences. She has taught me to enjoy a single flower growing at the foot of a cactus plant in the desert. Before meeting her I would have walked right past it and never notice it. Now, I enjoy each opportunity to see something as beautiful as a single red rose.

Chapter 7

Dash Actions:

1. Take every opportunity to enjoy people!
2. Take every opportunity to meet people!
3. Take every opportunity to serve people!
4. Take every opportunity to help people!
5. Make sure you get a chance to experience a different culture than your own!
6. Learn to see life through other people's eyes!
7. Look for the enjoyment in interacting with people!
8. Enjoy a red rose as often as the opportunity presents itself!

Chapter 8

CREATING A GREAT SUPPORT SYSTEM!

As I discussed in the last chapter, people are the most important thing after one's self when it comes to living life and creating a great Dash. In this chapter I would like to explore how important it is to have people in your life. We need our families for our daily support. We need all types of friends for supporting many different Dash situations. Let's start with a discussion on our family as an important part of our support system.

Family!

Your family is probably the most important people in the world for enhancing your Dash. As a young person I use to take family for granted. I would occasionally call my family members, but now that I have passed the big five-O, I truly value my family.

I lost my biological mother at the tender age of nineteen about a couple of weeks after I left home for the first time and joined the Navy. But, God is very fair and gave me a great step mother when my father remarried. She has now been my mother longer than my biological mother was my mother, before she died. My stepmother is the most awesome lady in the world. She is a champion of people. She is very aggressive in everything she does, but knows how to make that a positive part of her Dash for most people who encounter her. She can be very demanding, abrupt, controlling and even pushy, in her approach to accomplish what she wants to accomplish.

My mother (I will now drop the step, because it is no longer the way I think about her, she is my mother) has been one of the strongest forces in my life. She has been there for me when ever I have needed her. She has fascinated me in her ability to make things happen. I always say to her, it is too bad that all you ever wanted to be is a school teacher. I think you would have made a lot of money as the CEO of a Fortune 500 Corporation. She always reminds me that we need great school teachers or we would never have great CEO's. I have come to cherish and value school teachers and when I donate my personal time, it is usually to the public education system in America. My mother worked her way up through most of the positions you could have in the hierarchy of school administrators inside of a public school system. What I latched on to most about my mother is her love for people. Yes, sometimes her family suffered while she was helping others, but in the end we all benefited from her selflessness. We too have learned to work to help people when ever we can. Yes, my sister and I would say, she has loved us to the point that it hurted, but this has been rare. The hurt comes from not having more of her time. She is a superwoman. She was one of the best school teachers the world has ever seen, now being retired. She still works on special projects for the school system in America and continues to volunteer in public life and through her sorority.

My father was a teenage father and lived his young life some what vicariously. Today, my father is a nice old man and has learned to show his love for me in soft unique ways. He has some chronic diseases and they keep him home most of the time. At this time in my life I am glad to have him at the end of the phone every time I call and need to talk to him.

I have had nineteen brothers and sisters, six from my mother and thirteen from my father. Yes, I come from a once typical New Orleans family that has been influenced by Creole, French, Native American, European and African cultures. At this time in my life I have only lost one sister to cancer. I feel totally blessed to have so many brothers and sisters. I am close to my baby sister from my mother and that is only because she and I work hard at staying in touch. Interestingly enough we are the two that left home for many years to go out and see the world. Most of my brothers and sisters are still living in or near New Orleans and I only see them on rare occasions. To have family members alive and well is a great part of your Dash structure. If you are a person like me they don't need to do much more than be available to visit on holidays and special occasions. Having a family gives one purpose, belonging and heritage and this enhances the Dash experience, greatly. They are the village that we all need at some point in time in our lives. If you are fortunate enough to have them in your personal Dash support system, you are indeed a blessed person. Now, let's turn our attention to how children affect our Dash.

Before Children!

I have a premise about how our lives are divided and I am convinced that God gave us children to help us understand how it should be divided. It goes like this! Our life is segmented into three portions: There is a portion that comes before we have children; a portion that comes during the time our children are in our homes and finally, the portion that happens after our children leave home and, hopefully, stay away from home.

Let's discuss the portion before we have children. I know some of us never marry or don't have children for various reasons. For those of you that this is the case, you only get to experience this portion. Before we have children, this is a time of finishing your education and setting up your life the way you would like it to go. I have friends who have used this time to travel and see the world, especially after they were done with school and had good incomes. This is a good time to start working on your finances and setting things in motion to have workable finances. I love to council the very young and naïve about investing and building their wealth. You see, this is the time to be smart, cleaver and creative. This is the time you want to take your biggest risk in life. Children are not here to slow you down or make you second guess where you need to focus. The reality is that children affect our lives in some ways we can't often control. So this time without children can be a glorious time.

During my time before children, I joined the Navy to see the world. I met my wife in a part of the world I hadn't dreamed of seeing. Thanks to the GI Bill back in that day, I bought my first home. I then went to college and this time was ended by the birth of a beautiful daughter who arrived during my junior year in college.

I also have friends that are stuck in this segment of their lives simply because they can't have children. One set of my close casual friends have replaced not having children with keeping their two dogs. I think these are two of the most privileged dogs in the world. These dogs have everything a child could want and more. But, if my friends had their way they would love to have two kids. They tried to have kids by every avenue that was available to them and it was not meant to be. I once asked them why they didn't adopt. They answered, it was not their choice and we left the conversation there. They seem quite content taking care of their dogs. I suspect they will get a third dog one day.

During Children!

Once the kids come, you can't be quite as selfish as you use to be. You can't just take off alone, just the two of you, every other weekend to do something fun. I will tell you this, my wife and I have always had some sort of camper or trailer and this was a great way to spend time with our kids when they were very young. When we finally got to what is called a class-c coach which was thirty-two feet long, with separate beds for each of the kids and all the other amenities of a home, life was great. The motor home allowed us some freedom to really go and to stay in various places at an affordable cost. We traveled every inch of the western Pacific coast. We enjoyed the beauty of the coastline starting from Astoria, Oregon all the way down to Coronado Bay in San Diego, California and loved almost every minute of it. We and the kids have watched the sunset over the ocean from our beds.

Kids make life interesting! It is my belief that kids are a way God rewards us through biological nature. We procreate and reproduce ourselves. This can be exciting, scary and rewarding all at the same time. I loved raising my kids, but there were interesting challenges. My daughter was a peach to watch grow up - from "Dad why can't I get a boyfriend?" in seventh grade to "Dad, I am prepared for you to never speak to me ever again, because I am moving in with my boyfriend" - at the tender age of nineteen. Yes, she moved back home a year later after a traumatic experience. She is now happy and has embarked on college after what I call a four year delay to find herself.

My son on the other hand has cost me lots of dollars in court and juvenile hall fees in the state of California. He found drugs and bad friends and many of you know the rest of this story. At times, I truly lost control of my Dash due to him. He disappointed me and I let him know it in no small way. I am glad to let you know I got through this part of my Dash just fine and now I look back on it as a time of learning to build relationships when all is not easy. He has grown up not only to be good looking, but has aspirations of being a Chef and he has started to work towards that end and I am very proud of him. I still wonder what his final station in life will be, but I love him dearly. That's life with kids!

After Children!

Now for the good part, I am happy to say both of my children are out of the house and this is a great time in my life. I have the workable finances for continuing to enjoy my life. I have relatively, beautiful health. I have some great, casual friends. I have been married to the same woman, as you now know, for twenty eight plus years and yes, I am quite proud of this accomplishment. This life after children is awesome. The personal and selfish aspects of the Dash can be brought to the forefront for maximum pleasure at this time in your life.

You should see where I am sitting today. My children are miles away. The sky is billowy blue and the water is tropical marine green and I am somewhere in the orient. Awesome!

Darrell D. Simms

Life Long Friends!

Life would be totally unfinished without a life long friend. I have a friend name Jack, that I have written about already in this book and he has been my friend for over twenty-eight years. He and I met when I was only twenty-four years old, just as I was about to get married. A few years earlier he had finished a two year tour of duty in Viet Nam while serving in the Army and I had recently finished a four year tour of duty with the Navy. He and I met in the church. We were married about one year apart and we had our daughters about one year apart. I think you might say we had some things in common. As I said in an earlier section of this book, we never spend much time together, but when we do, it is high, quality time.

Jack and I have learned to place high value on our friendship over many years. The value comes from being able to pick up the phone and ask each others advice on subjects ranging from how to explain to our wives the next move we are trying to make in our finances and careers to how to keep our sons interested in school. We have encouraged each other and scolded each other on many occasions and we try to provide what ever emotional support that we can. I love Jack like a brother.

The love that comes from a deep friendship is awesome and hard to compare to the love of other relationships. It manifests itself in very low drama and continually exceeds all expectations. In other words - we make each others Dashes longer and more pleasant. Jack and I, both being God-fearing, strong family-oriented men have made our friendship an invaluable weapon that helps get us through the trying times of our lives. Our love for each other is brotherly in nature, but I feel much closer to Jack than any of my sibling brothers or sisters.

I go up to Seattle to visit him about 1 to 2 times a year, usually while I am on a business trip and he visits me about every three to five years, depending on where I am living. Our time together with each other and our wives is fantastic and leads to great experiences and memories.

As friendly as I am on a daily basis with people, I don't have many treasured friends. I do have some friends that I love to spend time with, but not like Jack. We once lived in the same city for about 11 years together and saw each other at least every few months, but we have never been the type of friends that require seeing each other on a daily or weekly or even a monthly basis. As I said earlier, we have enjoyed most of our time together, even if it is just an early morning telephone call to see how each other is doing. This type of friendship and relationship is invaluable to your Dash.

Casual Friends!

Whereas your life long friends are few and a very important part of your life; your casual friends make your day-to-day life great. These are the friends that you meet at work or at church or at the gym, etc. They come over to your house or you go over to their house on occasion and do fun things together. They are likely a part of your local Dash Club and you need them in your support structure. These are the friends that come and watch a movie with you or go out to dinner with you on paydays. These are people you enjoy and truly like to be around. They work to balance the friendship and are likely to pay for dinner as you would also do for them. They are the friends that will have you over for dinner on holidays and you will reciprocate as appropriate.

I am one who believes you need at least four to six of these friends, so you don't burn each other out. You may see these friends on a weekly to monthly basis. If you are married or a couple, you may have several couples in your Dash Club that fill this bill. You can swap off going out with these various couples and this keeps the friendships fresh and enjoyable.

It is very important to a healthy Dash that you maintain these types of friendships and they can change when certain circumstances change. For instance, you and your life-long friends will track each other for years and if necessary, track each other around the world. Your casual friends may come and go out of your lives when you change jobs or relocate to another city. I have been known to keep some of my casual friendships strong for years after I move from a location where I met them. I may be a bit unique in that I work very hard at choosing friends that are highly compatible with me and my family. That's right, I said I choose them and sometimes they choose me. My wife needs few friends, but I enjoy many friends and most of the time I think they enjoy me. I believe all friendships start out casual and some of them become life long friends.

I have a lot of casual friends at work and I truly enjoy eating lunch with them on occasion. One of the ways I make these friends is by asking them to take me to their favorite restaurant for lunch and usually I pay the first time out. This becomes one of the things we do together whenever possible. When I feel like eating a certain food for lunch I will think of a friend that likes that type of food and many times they reciprocate. I am elated when one of my friends calls me for lunch and I would not feel bad if they told me they felt like eating a meatball sandwich and thought of me. My friends all know I love meatball sandwiches. It really helps me get through my day when I have had a good lunch and stimulating conversation with one of my casual friends.

Again the casual friend should be a constant force in your life and is very important for enhancing your Dash.

Levels of Expectations for Friendships!

I think, the most important part of a friendship is what level of expectations gets set in the early part of the relationship. If those expectations are too high the friendship will suffer from one of the friends trying to meet the lofty expectations of the other. The friend that sets too high of an expectation will surely get disappointed. If one of the friends get disappointed, it is likely that he or she might quite possibly want to dissolve the friendship.

If you are the one setting those expectations, you may want to make sure they are at the right level. I like to always think of my friendships as highly two-way and mutual in benefits. I have had some one way friendships and I always felt as if I was being taken advantage of and therefore, ended those friendships. I believe I have been guilty of setting my expectations too high and making it hard for some my friends. I also know I have had friends who took total advantage of me and my family and they were not my friends once that was discovered. You setting the appropriate level of expectations usually guarantee that these friends become an important part of your Dash Club.

Chapter 9

Dash Actions:

1. Work hard to achieve as many goals as you can before you have children!
2. If you like to travel do some before your children come, it will be an enjoyable time of your life!
3. Enjoy your children, the time you have with them is shorter than you think!
4. Don't try to understand everything that happens to you with your children. Just live life the best you can!
5. Life is very beautiful after your children are gone!
6. Make as many life long friends as you can, they are in valuable!
7. Have as many casual friends as you can manage in you life!
8. Be nice to people!
9. Make your friendships beneficial to you and to your friends!

Chapter 9

WORKABLE FINANCES!

Some people say money is not everything and I would agree that the love of money is a problem for most of us mortals. But! Money is an important element in making a dark, deep, black, and lasting Dash. Our Dash, as you now know is a set of experiences that we will pass on to the next generation of family and friends and colleagues. Oh, by the way, in spite of Bill Gates not leaving his entire fortune to his children, because he thinks they can't handle it, your children would love for you to leave a little of your unused fortune for them. If things work out according to plans, I hope to leave my children quite a bit, but if not, they have received quite a bit already.

Setting up workable finances is truly where the rubber meets the road. You will not have that great car to make your drive to work a great experience or that fabulous house with the video theatre that seats six comfortably without a great financial plan. Workable finances are a must, if you are going to afford the great pleasures of life that you deserve. I have yet to get any material thing I want with out being able to pay for it. Even if something is gifted to you someone else has worked out the finances for it.

Yes, most of what this world offers is material. You are material (biological chemicals) worth about a $1.70 with inflation. There are people who believe that you should not focus too much on the material things of this life. I am here to tell them they lead a simple and dull life and I would probably guess, they wouldn't like me very much. I am the first to tell you, I like the finer things in life and I believe I deserve them as much as the next person. I have learned not to look at what Earl and Sarah Jones (The Jones's) have, but to have my own desires and they are enough to keep me motivated and working hard. As I said earlier, what makes America the place to live is that it provides us the opportunity to have great luxuries and pleasures. I want to drive the nicest car I can afford. I want to live in the nicest home I can afford. I want to take as many trips abroad as I can afford. I want to be able to give a way as much money as my heart desires and I can afford. Yes, the optimal thought and question here is - can you afford it? It equals material!

As I shared with you earlier, I have learned to "not just try, but to "Do!" This is the only way you are going to accomplish your goals or make something happen on your behalf or for your family and friends. Now with this premise being set, we can now discuss some of the planning, strategy and activities that must be executed if workable finances are going to be a part of your tool kit.

First and foremost you must have a good to great source of income. We will assume this will be a job that is based on education or a set of career experiences you have obtained over the years. I used to take a job for granted until I didn't have one for a time. I now clearly understand how important it is to find a good job on a stable basis. You must have a dependable income. The earlier you realize this; the better off you will be by the time you are in the middle of your Dash. Most of my life, I worked a job every day for a large, corporate organization. It afforded me and mines a great life. I made an above average American Family-wage. This was truly a good thing.

If you have already realized the American dream and found yourself fortunate enough to own your own company and make more money than you can spend, I am envious and still attempting to do that. America affords us this ability to create wealth in many ways. Work your finances and your finances will work for you and you will be happier.

Investing!

A job will get you so far, but is unlikely to get you to that great state of having finances that really allow you to live the life you really want to live. Many of us are content to live our lives in a very stable and low to no risk way, especially when it comes to our finances. My wife is one of those people. She is very conservative and always wants things to be even keeled. I often tell her, "If I was as stable conscious as you are, we would not have half the things we have acquired." If the truth be told, she would be fine with that, hence her stability. She would argue that she is a risk taker due to her putting a portion of her 401K retirement monies in the aggressive growth funds.

Most of us are willing to work hard and even save some money and are far too willing to go into financed debt to buy almost anything. Guilty as written! I have financed many of the material things I own. I seem to still be financing the cars we own. I have been one of those people that got into too much debt early in life. Yes, I am very proud after paying them off five to six years later. I am always sad when I see how much I really paid over the years in interest. I believed I could have bought two more cars with the interest I paid on cars. Today, I realize the errors of my ways and I am trying to leverage everything I can into aggressive growth funds.

(I am not a professional financial planner; I offer this information to make you think and seek the appropriate expertise.) I am now trying to use money to create wealth.

I have learned over the years, there are many things we can do to create wealth. One is investing in the stock market. Most people are afraid to invest in the stock market on their own. There are many books out there that will tell you how to get started and the basics of trading stocks. For most people that means buying low and selling high. Yes, buy the stocks when they are at their lowest price and sell them when they are at their highest price. This is not as easy as it sounds, but it is definitely not vary hard to learn. I have found that if you pick any ten stocks that have made it on to the New York Stock Exchange or the NASDAQ, that on average they will earn you no less than 10 percent over a five to ten year period. I first read this fact in a book. You simply get on the web and learn how to buy stocks from something like E-Trade or some other web based service and there are many others. You can Google and find all the information that you need to trade stocks or any other type of investing. If you don't know what Google is, go and ask one of your co-workers or family members. Don't stop asking until you find out, it will be one of the best tools you will ever learn to use in this day and age.

I believe at the time that I am writing this book that we are at the beginning of a new bull market cycle, which in most cases lasts ten years. If you are reading this book close to the time I published it, you need to be buying stock, they are at a low point and will do nothing but go up in value. You will be well on your way to creating some wealth in the stock market that will lead to some good workable finances. (Remember, I am not a professional, seek a professional for financial advice. I offer the following information to make you aware. Do your home work!)

Here are a few tips and hints:

1. Learn to use the internet to get information on stocks. Start with www.etrade.com . If you don't like that one, use the web to find another.

2. Learn how to look up a stock by using its symbol. An example is Microsoft; it trades under the symbol of MSFT.

3. Track a stock by watching how it trades and increases in value over time. Microsoft has risen in value over the last twenty years very significantly. That is why Bill Gates is the richest man in the world. It is based on his stock and its value. When tracking it, watch the press releases and how the company is being managed and what products the company is producing. Find out if it is profitable. All of this information is on the web.

4. Once you are convinced that it is a stock you want to buy and invest in, buy it on line using the tips I shared above. You only need about two hundred dollars to get started. I would suggest you buy no more than five hundred dollars if it is your first time. Yes, there is some risk of a stock going up and then back down. But, remember you are investing, not just rolling the dice in Vegas. You must let the money stay long enough to make money. If you do your homework you will learn what you need to know.

5. Then continue to watch the stock and watch your money grow. Remember, this is a long term investment (Years not days). I find it fun to log on to the web and watch the stock that I own. Yes, I have had stocks that did not perform well. I got rid of them and lost some money.

6. At some point in the future you will sell it and hopefully, if done correctly, you will make money!

Remember to do your home work, I am only telling you how I

have gained some of my workable finances. There are also financial planners out there who are willing to help you for a fee. Many of them can be quite good at what they do. Again, "do your homework," before letting someone else invest your money! Much of the information that these planners will have is available to you on the web. There are other things you can invest in but I don't have the time here in this book to tell you all the ways to invest your money. There are many books that are much better suited to help you in this quest of gaining wealth. I just want to make you aware of these strategies.

The ability to research an investment on the web is phenomenal. Do not underestimate the power of the web. It is a most powerful tool for dealing with your finances. From on-line banking to finding out how well a company is doing before you plop down your five hundred dollars or more for their stock. You can find out whether or not the CEO of a company kicks his dog or not before you invest in his company. (I shared that because as you know I have friends that love their dogs.) I am amazed at how much detailed information is available on the web. I am a very good user of technology, but I must admit you can spend a lot of time just going from fact to fact on the web and it can be an endless process. Just remember, the web is a financial tool and not the financial bible. There is just as much erroneous information out there as there is good and useful information. So, do your home work!

Another way of gaining some workable finances is by investing in property and owning a piece of the rock. America has had one of the most successful housing markets in its history over the last 30 years. It has afforded more than 50 to 60 percent of its population to have home ownership. This has afforded more Americans to accumulate some significant wealth due to home equity. This has allowed Americans to achieve a level of financing that has led to significant purchase of rental and vacation homes and other material wealth that has never been seen before in the history of the country. Add the dot.com era to this and Americans are living extremely well. They have learned to take the equity out of their homes and propagate it to a number of other investments that lead to a pretty nice life in the United States.

Retirement!

From a Dash perspective, retirement is the ultimate plateau to reach. My definition of retirement is working out your finances that allows you to wake up in the morning and do exactly what you want to do and not what you have to do to put food and water on the table. If you are in your twenties reading this book, you are intelligent and motivated enough to probably retire when you are in your forties. I don't mean I am giving you all the answers, but I know you are thinking about how to better your life. The positive thinking that goes along with reading a book like this qualifies you to be in this exclusive club.

It is never too early to get started working on your finances that will allow you to retire. As I have stated earlier in this chapter, we are in one of the nicest economic growth times for the century. The stock market is bullish, the interest rates are still low and the job market is growing. The housing market is cooling off at a nice pace and housing starts are up. This makes the United States a great place to make money and having enough money is what leads to retirement.

Retirement preparations start with your 401k and please, please learn how to monitor this investment. Yes, you can use the web to watch this investment. Your 401k is one of the most important investments you will ever make. Many people allow their employer to go in and take money out of their salaries and put it into their 401k plans and then they forget about it. You don't put money into your check book or savings account and forget about it. The internet allows you to watch your 401k at will, on a daily basis if you wish. I am a firm believer that investments are like gardens. The more you prune, de-weed and water them the more they flourish. I taught my wife to watch her 401k and now she is like a mad woman, moving her funds around. She gets very excited every time she makes a new thousand dollars. During this writing she is growing her investment by 30% a month. She now enjoys watching the progress of this investment. If you understand what the funds are doing and how they are being managed and you now know why to invest in them, it becomes very exciting. Due to the internet, you can be more aggressive with your 401k. Set limits and stick to your plans. Most 401k plans will let you move your money on a daily basis although that is not a good idea. Make sure you understand the hidden cost that might be there for certain transactions. And always remember when to cut your losses. Many people lost hundreds of thousands of dollars because they were not watching their investments when the stock market crashed during the "dot-bomb." They didn't bail out when they should of, hoping their investments would suddenly turn around and come back. Remember this most important thing – history is the best indicators for when to get in and out of markets. The 401k is an investment not an account where an employer just deposits funds for you.

Properly managed investments will make sure you have the workable finances you need to buy that place on the beach in the Philippine Islands. Hopefully, you will need a place where you can spend some of that retirement time and money and finish out your Dash in style.

Chapter 9

Dash Actions:

1. In order to live a good life you must make your finances work!
2. Get a good source of income!
3. Invest your money whenever possible to create wealth!
4. Seek good financial planning advice as early in life as you can understand to do it!
5. Watch and manage your 401k Retirement Plan and other investments on the web!
6. Plan for retirement early in life!
7. Invest! Invest! Invest!

Chapter 10

OWNING A PIECE OF THE ROCK!

Plymouth Rock - where ownership started in the U.S. was the start of something big. I have had the opportunity to work and make a decent salary in the high-tech world. This salary along with some smart investing has allowed me to own quite a few things. I have often been heard saying, if you want to lower crime in America, then help people to own a piece of the rock. This ownership doesn't stop with just a home. This goes back to that thinking process I outlined earlier. If a person thinks in a positive way, they will make positive things happen. A mindset of ownership is a totally positive mindset. "I own it and so I will treasure and protect it."

In an earlier book, I attempted to answer a question of why did people destroy all that property during the aftermath of the Rodney King Verdict. The answer was simple; they lost hope for where their Dash was headed and the bigger issue was they didn't own it. When you don't own something or have no hope of owning it, you are more likely to take any opportunity to destroy it. Most of the wars of this world have this same premise behind them. They destroy all that is in their path because they don't own it. The people who are on the defense work hard to fight their enemy and preserve their land, their beliefs and their lives.

In our world of Dash thinking we want to control our destiny and therefore, if you want to control the use of assets, you must own them. If they are your assets they are usually under your control. Once you have ownership this leads to a possessive thinking and that thinking usually leads to a need to protect and grow the asset. This is especially true if we are talking about stocks or real estate property.

There is no greater feeling than that of the anticipation that comes with the realization that you can afford to acquire the asset that you desire. What is equally as fun is the entire journey that leads up to making the acquisition or purchase. When making a large purchase such as a home, the excitement can be over whelming and exhilarating.

Buy a House!

One of the best ways to own a piece of the rock is by buying and investing in property. We all need a place to lay our heads every night. There are usually three ways to get that place. The first is to have a great family that provides for you. The second is to rent a place. The third is to buy a residence. Buying and owning your own place is one of the best things that you will ever do once you can afford to make it happen.

I remember having a thousand dollars in the bank just after leaving Uncle Sam's Navy. I had the GI bill in my back pocket. The bill was a guarantee to all banks in the United States that if they loaned me money the government would guarantee to pay it back, if I couldn't. There are still programs of a similar nature to help first time buyers get their first house.

I remember meeting with the realtor and telling her I wanted to buy a house and I had a thousand dollars in the bank and that wonderful GI Bill. Skeptical, she smiled at me and my wife and said she would help us if she could. She came back a few days later and showed us several houses that we could afford to buy. They weren't very big and they weren't very new, but they were affordable and nice. We hopped in her car and looked them over and by the end of the day had made a choice.

I will never forget how exciting it was to become a homeowner and to own a piece of the rock in the United States of America. From a Dash point of view, I was always proud to go out and cut my grass. Today, I don't have to cut grass. Ah, the evolution of a good Dash. Due to having achieved workable finances, I have a lawn care guy who does that for me. I am too busy doing all my other fun things with my free time on the weekend. Over several more years, I bought two more homes from her, until she finally retired. That first home we bought from her, we owned for nearly twenty years, although we only lived in it for about two years. At one time we owned three homes. I was also able to offer my brother a place to live for about five years before he bought his first home. My Dash grew thicker from these great experiences.

I have had the opportunity to build a dream home from the ground up. I remember buying the property two years before I had the resources to build a house on the property. It turns out it wasn't very far from the home I was currently living in. I used to walk my doggy up the hill and sit looking out at the Oregon Olympic Mountain Range and dream of the day I could build the house. After owning the property for two years it increased in value by about fifty percent. The bank was willing to lend me all the money I needed to build the house with no down payment. We were able to build a four thousand square foot home with three levels. It was truly a dream home. But get this, we wrote off most of the interest on the house for many years, because my wife used it during the day for her daycare business. For eleven years she served over thirty families. We paid very little taxes for nearly five years through depreciating the house as a business expense for the daycare service. We made about one hundred thousand dollars when we sold it five years later. This is how you get workable finances and be able to perpetuate them. I have always made significant money on buying and selling houses over the years. When it comes to buying and selling property – "Time is Money." Making money is a good use of Dash time and creates a quality Dash.

Buy a Getaway!

I have had the opportunity to own two places for recreational pupuses. One was in the mountains of Washington State and the other was on the Oregon Coast. At both places, I have had many, many years of great fun with my wife and kids on holidays and weekends. I still own the one on the Oregon Coast. It is now simply an investment property. Eventually, I will sell it and make money on it. Remember, money spent in the right place over time will grow into more money.

All of this comes from having workable finances and it feeds back to increasing your finances by creating wealth through investing. Any kind of deeded land in America will grow in value in America if it is in the right location.

As you know by now, my wife is from the Philippines. During this writing we bought some land on the Island of Cebu in the Philippines and built a nice getaway on the white sanded beaches. The property cost me fifty grand and another twenty grand to refurbish it with full direct access to the beach. I have learned to think outside of the box and live life to the fullest. I may never go back to Hawaii for a vacation again, with the Philippines now having such rich experiences waiting and at a more affordable cost. These are the experiences that contribute to a long, dark, solid Dash.

Buy a Great Car!

I wrote this section while I was waiting for my wife to join me in the Lexus dealership. Again, at the risk of sounding a bit materialistic and selfish, I cannot encourage you enough to one day buy that dream car. I have been fortunate to have driven a beautiful, although used 1988 Jaguar XJ6. You may remember it was on my list of ten goals to accomplish. It wa a treasure.

It is amazing how much time we spend in our cars driving back and forth to work or driving around on the weekend. Driving your car should be great quality time and one way to make it quality time is to ride in the car of your choice. I can't tell you how much I enjoyed driving my XJ6 for the twelve years I had it. It did cost me a few headaches in keeping up the maintenance. Now thinking back on it, it was worth every penny and every minute I spent working on it.

While writing this book I bought the second car of my dreams. Yes, Yes, Yes, an Infiniti G-35 sedan. It is a great car and I got my favorite color, dark blue. Even though many people told me that the black interior would be hot in the Arizona summers. I bought black interior. Yes, it is hot, but once the air condition kicks in I look and feel as cool as I thought I would. Everyone who rides with me has a pleasant experience on that black interior once the air conditioner gains control.

But, get this, I was coming out of a supermarket one day and headed into the parking lot. A woman looked me over and then carefully asked, "Is that your Infiniti?" I answered, "Yes" and smiled with great pride. Then she said, "I thought so with you being dressed so classy. I bought a Honda last year; I really want to get an Infiniti. How do you like it?" My answer led to a twenty minute dissertation on Infiniti G-35 cars. What a feeling to have some one validate your choice in such a manner. She was totally shocked when I offered her a test drive. She declined, but did sit in the driver's seat for a moment. I came home and shared the story with my wife and never stopped smiling while finishing this section of the book.

Hopefully, by now you have bought into how valuable time is and how important it is to spend it wisely. If you can sit back in a great car and listen to your favorite music, you are enjoying life, making great use of time and darkening your Dash.

Oh, as for my wife who likes to call me selfish, yes, she walked out of the Lexus dealership with a Lexus RX 300, used, but with all the amenities that you can get in that car. She feels quite blessed when she is riding her thirteen miles to work at 6:30 am in the morning and sipping her mocha from Starbucks.

Chapter 10

Dash Actions:

1. Understand that ownership is a great privilege in America!
2. You should work towards owning everything you possibly can!
3. Drive the car you want and can afford!
4. Enjoy every minute of your ownership and build an inheritance for your children!
5. Don't focus on the material aspects of ownership, but do focus on the enjoyment of what you have!

Chapter 11

GAINING AND KEEPING YOUR HEALTH!

One of the things that will keep your deathday away for as long as possible is good health. It is unfortunate that we don't understand the value of our health until it is late in life or we don't have it. In America, most of us take for granted the ability to go see a doctor, almost at will. We live our lives knowing if something happens to us, someone will call 911 and in minutes some highly trained medical technicians are going to be there to take care of us. This is not good Dash thinking.

I would like to shift this thinking and the paradigm that goes with it. What if we go back and think of the Dash on the tombstone and find ways to not be the foundation for that tombstone just yet. To change our thinking to "how precious this life is to each of us and start to treat our bodies as if they need to last forever." To fully value our heart, our brain, our joints and our abilities to do the simple things like walking.

I was sitting in the Chicago O'Hare Airport today and I was doing my normal people watching while listening to some smooth Jazz by Wayman Tisdale the ex-Phoenix Sun and now a great jazz bassist. You need to know us writers like airports and airplanes. Thanks to the advent of the laptop they are very conducive to good bouts of writing. Anyway, I was watching a woman and I believe she was with her daughter. The woman was sitting and eating some fruit and that seemed a healthy act. She looked as if she was in much pain. She then finished her fruit and then got up and using a cane she walked to the restroom. She winced as she got out of the chair and ambled slowly to the restroom with a little assistance from another woman who appeared to be a close relative. She came back to sit with her traveling companion and slowly fell back into her seat.

I deduced that she was at least fifty to sixty pounds over weight especially for her height. Here companion was also 30 to 40 pound overweight. I thought to myself, if I was that much over weight and in that much pain; I would get my stomach stapled today. I don't write this lightly, I felt sorry for her and would have loved to council her on her weight. She was not enjoying life and definitely did not have any good Dash thinking when it came to her health. The proof was right in front of me; she was not taking good care of herself. I would encourage you to be very serious about taking care of your health. Your weight is the first place to start.

I am a "die for the look" girl watcher and I stopped noticing all the pretty women and started counting how many people were overweight. It was disheartening. America is too fat and we will pay for this in Dash length and depth. Now with all that sadness expressed let's move back to where we need to be: The Solution.

Preventive Maintenance!

We need to put our bodies on a preventive maintenance program just like we do with our cars and other appliances in our possession. We should not wait until we break ourselves before we think about fixing ourselves, because it takes a lot longer to fix ourselves once they are broken. Many parts of our body, once broken, can often be irrepairable. We often take better care of inanimate objects than we do ourselves. I too have been guilty of this neglect. The ability to keep healthy continues to get easier and easier in America. One day we are going to pass that national health bill and catch up with the rest of the world. In the mean time we need to focus on self.

First and foremost we need to get back to walking. How often do you see people walking in America? I remember when I was a kid, we walked everywhere. I must admit, we did it out of necessity, having no money to do the alternatives. I love to walk and I walk as often as I can and all my walking is not planned exercise. I play golf at least once a week and walk as often as I can and I take every opportunity to walk.

At work, I don't call people; I walk to see and talk to them face to face. I agree, this is not as productive for accomplishing more and more work, but we work too much any way as I will discuss later. As I said earlier, I spend a lot of time in airports. I try not to ride the people moving walkways all the time; I will get on the carpet and hump my way to the terminal. I smile as I am doing it and I am very proud when I get to where I am trying to go. I also use the time as a clear thinking exercise.

When I go to the store or mall, I try to park out in an unpopulated area of the parking lot. This encourages me to walk a little further. Not only is this good for my cardio, it is also good for decreasing the dents in my nice car. No, I am not paranoid. I like me and my car and preventive measures are far less expensive than the alternative.

I read many articles on how walking helps the body, I recently read an article that says walking helps to stave off the decreasing of our memory capability. I just like the feeling I get from walking. It is such an accomplishment to complete any kind of walk. In this day and age I wonder if any of us can run very fast, if we had to run for our lives. Even I think I might get winded after some big sprint. There are those of us who have running regiments and I applaud you or any of you who have good routine exercise programs. Next we have to change our eating habits.

America is eating its way into bad health. I have a philosophy now, which says if my body doesn't want it, I don't need it and therefore I don't eat it. All of us know that ice cream is a great treat at any time. My body is lactose intolerant. I have been told by people you are missing a lot out of life by not eating ice cream. Some people have even encouraged me to take a pill that will allow me to eat ice cream. I think it would be absurd to take a pill in order to eat ice cream and make my body do something that is not healthy for it. I was well into my adult life before realizing that I was lactose intolerant. The symptoms were clear; I would get bloated and gassy and feel slighted nauseated and was not so good to be around. No more, I simply don't eat the stuff and I am better for it.

My body also doesn't like chocolate; I will get pimples and zits if I eat chocolate, but don't feel too sorry for me I get my share of pleasures in many other ways. I have had colleagues that bought chocolate cake for my birthday and I didn't eat any of it. I did enjoy watching everyone else celebrate my birthday by enjoying a bite of cake on my behalf. Do you realize how much sugar and fat you will miss if you take ice cream and chocolate out of your diet? Get this, I once worked for several years beside a chocoholic who lived for chocolate and on many occasion I contributed to her passion. For me, chocolate is not necessary, but I enjoyed seeing her enjoy it.

What you should know is that I have taught myself through discipline to not want any of that stuff. As I shared earlier, I get my share of sorbet on occasion. I have a passion for almonds and dried mangoes, cherries, pineapple and other such things. These are great snacks for me and they satisfy my sweet tooth. They are low in fat, but not always low in sugar. I drink a lot of orange juice and I try to eat things that are green, red, orange and other fruits and vegetables with good nutrients.

I am an advocate for watching what you eat all the time, so it becomes a habit and not a nuisance. Many times we forget

Pavlov's Dynamic Training Techniques; we are creatures of habits and routines. We can be trained to do the right things for ourselves. The best routines are those around good diet and exercise. The big, new news is; to keep your weight in check you must manage your caloric intake. Don't eat too much! Don't create habits of bad dietary practices. Eat in moderation.

If you are overweight already, you should immediately do something about it. Don't procrastinate to lose the weight that will contribute to bad health and eventually shorten your Dash. I am of the mind that we give away too much of our lives to our whims and what I call "living for the moment." Many people think, "I will just eat a little of this" and then they eat the whole thing. It is about control as a member of the Dash Club. If you lose control, then you will pay for it in some other way. Many times, life is a zero sum game and you don't get something for nothing.

Good health is predicated on good practices. When you encounter a problem with your health, you should immediately do all you can to fix the problem. Sometimes due to our finances there are tradeoffs, but they should be minimized when it comes to maintaining our health. To have your Dash penalized and neglected due to your neglect is a Dash sin, literally. I treat my health as one of my most prized possessions. For those of you, who have controlled and good health practices, enjoy what you have and keep working for the perfection.

The Prize of Good Health!

I believe you should treat your health as if it is a prize to win and keep. I think you should strive for it under all circumstance. I am one who advocates for people to have access to good healthcare. In the Dash way of thinking, life is based on good managed healthcare and we should be willing to do all we can to maintain it, at all costs.

Occasionally, I will have these debates with myself on how I value things. I have tried to prioritize what I would be willing to live without if faced with an unfortunate choice. Here is my thinking. I think I would never want to lose my eyesight. I think I would give up everything else before giving up my eyesight. I have a friend who is blind. He has been blind almost from birth. I have observed him enjoying life more than I have at times and he most certainly accomplishes as much as I do in life, as far as our career aspects are of concern. He is a jogger and he attaches himself to a sighted runner via a bungee cord and off he goes for a five mile jog. He is a great runner.

I have thought about what if I had to give up my hearing and what I would miss. I play saxophone and I play mostly by ear. I love music, especially the uniqueness of the sounds of the instruments. I need to hear in order to play. I don't know if you have ever had the experience of hearing Jean Luc Ponte and Stanley Clark and Al DiMeola play together. We are talking about three of the best jazz string artists in the entire world. Even now I can close my eyes and hear Jean Luc do things with a violin no person on earth can do. Stanley Clark can thump an upright bass beyond our imagination. This is when I know I have to have all my senses for as long as I can have them and I hope it is until they write my final epitaph.

As an avid golfer I need my arms and legs to golf. I can't imagine not being able to play golf. Golf doesn't only provide for good exercise, but I enjoy the beauty of the golf course settings. I need my eyes, because I love to take pictures of the scapes and views when golfing an ocean course or a mountain course or a desert course. I spend more of my leisure time on a golf course than on any other venue. All of my senses are totally stimulated while I am on a beautiful golf course in a beautiful place. It is just an awesome experience.

What about my nose and mouth? I was eating in a particular restaurant; I noticed on the wall there was the following saying:

"One cannot think well, love well, live well, if one has not dined well!"

Darrell D. Simms

I love to eat food from around the world. I have eaten Peking duck in China. I have eaten Kimchi in Korea. I have eaten sautéed shrimp in Singapore. I have had fish in the South of France. I have had coho salmon in Seattle. I have had pizza in Italy. I have eaten pancit noodles in the Philippines and of course, I have had the best food ever in my home town of New Orleans. No, I can't live without my nose and mouth, either. Food is a life long experience and that is what living is all about.

The prize of good health is the prize of living life to the fullest and making your Dash an extraordinary experience. Yes, it comes down to not being able to live without any of the things God has given us to enhance this short time here on earth. You had better treasure and value them or they may not serve you well.

But! If I lost them all, I would still work with what was left and work to enjoy life in any way I could. The worst lost of all is the lost of precious life, itself. For those of you, who have lost parts of your body due to unfortunate incidents, please know that I hope and pray that you continue to live life as best you can and that your Dash is still an extraordinary event in time.

Chapter 11

Dash Actions:

1. Value your health beyond anything else, it is a precious and rare asset and it is the essence of your life!
2. Take good care of yourself, it is the only one you will ever have!
3. The sooner you understand the value of your health the more valuable you health will become!
4. Watch your weight!
5. Practice good health as often as you can!
6. Be discipline in taking care of your health!
7. Take a walk everyday!
8. Take time to smell the roses!

Chapter 12

FOUNDED SPIRITUALITY IS A MUST!

Somebody once made me think of who I am and what makes me, me. She was a young lady that had no idea how she would change my life forever. Basically, she shared her faith with me while giving me my driver's license after I came back from serving in the military. Today, I can't thank her enough.

Founded – this is not just the spiritual part that comes from just being born. This is the part that comes from seeking a maker and finding a purpose for your life. This is achieving a relationship with God and having him acknowledge that relationship back by giving you his unmerited favor which we born again Christians call "Grace." But I am not here to sermonize you. I am here to encourage you to do all you can to live a great life while you are here on this earth and your spirituality should be an important part of your life.

A Must Have!

For some of you who read this book, this will be a chapter you skip and that is okay with me. My hope is that, this book will make you think about how important life is and what a precious gift it is to you. If you accept the premise that it was given to you in some manner by a higher power, then I am happier for you than if you don't.

I am a strong believer in God Almighty and that all life

comes from Him. It is a gift that is so precious; God will eventually change it into something even better. I believe that the body is a temple for a spirit and that spirit is also a gift from God. Without the spirit of God, the body is simply a limp piece of flesh that will start to decay in a matter of minutes and continue to decay until there is nothing left. I am talking about the spirit that gives us the gift of life.

You don't need to believe in God to get this gift from God – in my way of thinking. You simply get it and then you have some choices about what you do with it while you have it. This is where I believe Founded Spirituality is a must have. You can go through this life one day at a time. You can be materially wealthy, physically healthy, but spiritually dead and I won't push theology at you, just a few practicalities to make you think about this much needed spirituality that I am advocating you must have to complete your Dash.

Many people have everything they need in life when it comes to material wealth, but they still come up empty and lead self-professed miserable lives. They still search for Joy, Peace, Lasting Happiness and all the things I think that comes with founded spirituality. They still seek a relationship that is spiritual with a maker that made them for Himself and His purpose. At some point in your life you will want to be able to explain why you were put upon this earth and why you exist today. I think for some of us this comes with experiencing a mid-life crisis.

The whole idea of ceremoniously preparing a dead body to be returned to dust or ashes is an acknowledgement of the life it lived and now needs to be return to its origin. I have seen so many people who seem to have no purpose in life and they seem to not have much of a life. I am not here to judge anyone, but I am a casual observer of people's lives. I love people and I believe all that I do in life is done for people. I believe people are my main business. Here is an interesting question; do you grow a tomato just to see how big and luscious of a tomato you can grow? I believe you grow a tomato to be enjoyed by you or someone else through all the senses that you can bring to enjoy the tomato. I believe God grew you for his enjoyment, like you grew the tomato, to later enjoy you in a spiritual manner. Here is another take on what I am trying to communicate.

It is a lot of fun to be able to write a one to two hundred page book in about a six month period of time. When I am writing a novel, I so enjoy making the story happen, but I more enjoy when someone walks up to me and say I truly enjoyed reading your book. I am even more pleased when they pick a point in the book and can readily have a discussion about what my thoughts were on writing that particular part of the book. I believe God is pleased when you acknowledge back to him you understand the purpose for your life and that that purpose is to please him. I believe Founded Spirituality truly enhances life for you and the people that will experience you.

I can't tell you how complete my life is because of my belief in God almighty. When I think of an adoring God, it enhances the things that I do and experience. When I walk a golf course, I appreciate the pretty pink flowers that grow up out of a set of Lilly pads in a shimmering lake. (I have a great photo of them.) When I see a group of birds that all have black spots around their necks and their breasts are totally brown and their legs are lemon yellow and those markings appear in the exact same place on each of them, I see God. They all look exactly alike to my eyes and I am in awe of God. I am at a point in my life when I can't pass a beautiful flower or plant without acknowledging its beauty and attributing that to a creation by God. When I see a herd of wilder beasts running and making a sharp turn all in unison; this is all awesome stuff and allows me to be in total awe of God.

The human mind was meant to be in awe of things. Our brains experience such euphoric highs from this type of activity. This is the type of experience that leads people to be high on life. There is no better feeling than the euphoric high that is induced by living life itself and giving the credit of creation to God. This is what I call honoring and acknowledging God for what he has created. People who don't understand what I am talking about, in my opinion are not living life to the fullest, I am convinced of it.

I can't tell you how centered and grounded this belief makes me. I have been blessed with material wealth, and now more importantly, I am blessed with spiritual wealth. This is what I believe puts life in perspective and allows me to truly control my destiny. I have been known to say, even if there isn't a real God, the shear belief in God is enough to keep the world a great place for us silly, drama seeking human beings.

To fully make Founded Spirituality work for you, I propose a few steps you can take:

1.) Find a way to surround and fellowship with people who have your same beliefs. This leads to the biggest connection with other people that you will ever make.

2.) Take time to think about who you are and what your purpose for being on this earth is. I am here to tell you, you have one.

3.) In the Christian World we pray to our God and Creator. This is time taken to communicate with a higher power that helps us find our purpose in life.

4.) I believe you need to be a part of an organization that helps you grow in what you believe.

5.) Realize that the spirit within you, that gives you life, needs nurturing by something greater than just your thought process.

I understand that everyone doesn't believe the same way I do and that this chapter may be one that you don't agree with. I will allow you to be selfish and find your own way here. I believe that's the way my God wants it! You have the freedom to choose what you believe and that in it self is life changing.

Chapter 12

Dash Actions:

1. Put your faith in something bigger than a human!
2. Seek Peace in all that you do!
3. Find time to meditate on your purpose in life!
4. Enjoy a belief in a power that defines who you are!
5. Seek the spiritual power that completes your being here!

Chapter 13

ALL WORK AND NO PLAY IS
UNACCEPTABLE!

If you thought some of the earlier chapters of this book are my soap boxes for expressing my thoughts to the world, than this chapter will really get you going. I believe we Americans have come full circle when it comes to enjoying life. I believe that we have figured out how to work harder and how to work more productive and how to work smarter, but we have not figured out how to work less. We work too much!

I use to work twelve hour days and think nothing of it. I have colleagues that work fourteen hour days and think nothing of it. They call home and offer shallow excuses to their family as to why they are missing some important family event for the sake of making more money. One of my colleagues and a casual friend didn't know there were kids in his neighborhood. He never went home during the daylight to see them playing, until he had a discussion with me about the Dash. After our discussion he left work early one day and realized there were kids in his neighborhood and he had been living in that neighborhood for over two years. Even today, he still works long hours, although now I am happy to report he is taking more time off to enjoy life with me on some weekends.

In our commerce and business world of today, we all spend a lot of time dealing with our international counterparts. When I worked in the corporate world, people would get very upset when we needed to have some assistance or information from abroad and there was no one available to provide that assistance or information. I have heard people just go crazy because our Asian colleagues were on holiday at the time we thought we needed them. I have seen people get down and out during the late summer months because they know our European colleagues take what we would deem a significant amount of time off for holiday vacation.

Are we nuts here in America and have we become productivity fools? We make more money than we can spend and we don't take time off to spend it. I am personally here to put a stop to this. I warned you that I would be on a soap box. I think we had better stop and take time to have a cup of tea before we export it to China. We had better take time to drive all those cars we are exporting to Taiwan from our highly productive assembly lines. We had better take the time and play some of the golf courses we are designing for Viet Nam, Malaysia and China.

My best buddy that I work with gets some six weeks of vacation and he never uses it all. There are now policies in corporations that state, if you don't use all of your vacation, you will lose your vacation. Get this, vacation is also used as PTO (personal time off) for illness. We won't even take the time to recuperate from illness. This is a fringe benefit that we are now not taking full advantage of, how sad! When they send out the compensation sheet, they heavily emphasize your vacation as a part of the compensation package and we are now giving it back. They will take it back and give you nothing for it. Not only will they take it back, we are allowing ourselves to pressure each other not to take our vacation. Ridiculous!

Not only are corporations not encouraging you to take your vacations, they are making it difficult for you to take your vacation. You know what? It is not only their fault. It is also your fault, when you allow the work culture to do this to you. Yes indeed, I am guilty right along with you. Your management team has the same problem as you do. They are slaves to their own policies, rules and objectives. They are right along side of you perpetuating the problems. Here is the really sad part of this. Once it is a part of the work culture and hence, the social culture, it becomes very difficult to change. Everyone walks around feeling guilty that they want to take some time off to be with their family. We are now building into our culture to feel bad about taking our vacation. People are dreading their time off and they know their work will continue to pile up until they are back at their desk. All of our productivity tools that we invented in the twentieth century are holding us hostage in the twenty first century, such as, Email!

E-mail goes on vacation with most of us. I know people that go to Hawaii and continue to answer email for fear they are going to get snowed under or miss an opportunity. You know what? They are right! I have been guilty, before coming to my senses. I am still guilty of reading and answering email on weekends. The work week now starts on Sunday night for a lot of us. We start reading the email from Asia and Europe on Sunday nights to keep up with the international game.

The laptop now has its own place in our baggage and allows work to tag along on our vacations and time off. I am getting angry just writing about it. Almost every third person is carrying a laptop when I go through the security check point at the airport and get this; my excuse for taking my laptop on vacation is to use it as the repository for my pictures I take while I am on vacation. I can take hundreds pictures and view them at night on that dreaded vacation killer. After viewing the pictures, I have this silly thought, "let's just check email and see how many there are. Two hundred! Oh my God! I had better read some of them." After reading two hundred emails, you are too tired to enjoy that water fall and spa up the Columbia Gorge in Oregon. Don't worry somebody in your family got the pictures while you were sleeping. There is even one of you snoring during the drive pass the spectacular water falls. It is on your laptop. What about that other piece of hi-tech that has found its way onto our hip or into our purse. The Ubiquitous Cell

Phone!

The cell phone is truly the destroyer of a vacation. I have been guilty of calling a colleague on vacation knowing he spent the last six months with no real time off. I called him in the name of helping him manage his accounts while he was away. A crisis flares up two days after he is out of the office and immediately we are all dialing his cell phone hoping he will answer, so he can find one of the files he has on his laptop. Is this crazy or what? All these things we have invented in the name of productivity, has led to being ball and chains on us, when it comes to enjoying life. Don't forget how we don't have time to listen to jazz and reflect on our day as we drive home. Annnnh! We are on the cell phone!

We are very productive and I remember when I was studying time management in my Industrial Engineering course work, we were told this would lead to more time for leisure. What a farce and duping of society. We are decreasing the work staff in the name of cutting expenses due to trying to increase margin and profits. We now are short staffed and the only thing I see getting choked is vacation. Ok! Ok! Enough! I know you get the picture, but this is a Dash Club killer.

This year I put a stop to this by going on vacation in Asia. Yes, I was one of those people who they couldn't find. I did have my laptop for the picture repository, but I did not read any email for over fourteen days. I broke the cultural mold. I couldn't get to voice mail on my cell phone and only one night did it ring while I was sleeping and of course, I did not answer it!

Are you smiling, smirking or frowning as you think through this. Next question, are you guilty. If you are then join me in stopping it! This workaholic syndrome that so chronically affects our lives on a daily basis is one we can change. In case you forgot, we are talking about how we improve our Dash.

Conundrum of Commitment!

I have a great friend and member of my local chapter of

the Dash Club, his name is Gregg Kusmann. He shared with me how busy his wife was with her work, as he explained why she couldn't take any time off to accompany him to play golf with me and my wife. Being the great lady she is, she did let him break away alone to play with us. While sharing and explaining to me the situation, he asked me a most profound question and answered it. He said do you know the "Conundrum of Commitment?" That is what my wife is facing at this time in her business, things are great, but she is overwhelmed with work due to the boom in the housing market. By the way this was a Labor Day holiday weekend.

This is often the dilemma many of us find ourselves in, we are so busy making money, we don't have much time to spend it or use it to play. We are committed to work and we don't know how to get out of it. When we are not working, we are committed to improving our lives by working some more. Yes, we are committed to having all that we need in life accept living life it self. I know you have the feeling of being overwhelmed by what needs to be done. Do to societal norms; I think women are put into this situation more than men. Our society creates this conundrum. We men will lounge around the house after cutting the grass. Women will clean and cook and prompt and priss and must and fuss over everything. My wife spends hours doing her nails, dying her hair and prepping clothes for the next day. These are not necessarily my clothes, they are often hers. I often wash and iron my own shirts. And don't let us have guest over for an evening, she never sits down, even when the food is brought in by pot luck. She is often up cleaning the kitchen for a couple of hours after I have settled in front of the TV. Yes, I call her and remind her we are post children and no one will know the dishes are in the dish washer and haven't been washed yet. When we started using paper plates I thought all that work would be over.

We commit too much to things that take away precious time from ourselves and from our family and friends. If you don't agree than write me an email and explain it to me! (I will admit I have a righteous smile on my face as I am writing this section.)

I am kicking the habit and enhancing my Dash.

Entertaining You, First!

By now you have figured out, I love life and take this Dash Club stuff very seriously. I think, if you learn to entertain yourself first, then you will be an exciting person to know. If you learn to live for and with all the people around you, what a great life you will have and what a great life others will have because of you. This is where I want to encourage you to just have fun in every aspect of your life. If you take time to make sure you are living your life to the fullest, then the chances are you are promoting others to live full lives as well.

Prepare To Party!

My casual friends in our personal Dash Club are learning every day to spend money and time on pure fun and good living. Most of our club members love jazz and we have a smooth jazz radio station in Arizona that really knows how to bring on the party. They often sponsor great concerts. Throughout the year we attend these concerts and see some of the best jazz artists in the world. I will let you in on a little secret: Arizona's ticket prices for these events are so reasonable; we buy them at the drop of a hat and don't even think about the cost.

Now what do I mean by "prepare to party." You need to plan to enjoy more of your day-to-day life and absolutely live for your weekends. Our club now has a tradition of having a home cooked meal at least once a month. We rotate it so that it is only about once a quarter that you host everyone in your home. We all have exceptionally nice homes here in the desert and we do eat well. All of our wives are exceptionally good cooks. One of my friends spent several years in Italy and became a passionate wine connoisseur. He has a chiller where he stores his excellent wine collection. Now get this! I don't drink wine because of my own

Darrell D. Simms

religious beliefs and disciplines. But I thoroughly enjoy hearing my friend tell the rest of us the back story on each bottle of wine he introduces to us. And, it makes me happy to see them enjoy the wine as we enjoy each others company. These dinners add so much to our quality of life. They lead to some very wonderful times together.

We have a high tech Karaoke machine and one of my friends loves to ham it up on the machine. We never knew how good a singer he was until the machine showed up. He totally enjoys singing on the Karaoke microphone. We enjoy watching him mimic entertainers like Louie Armstrong as he sings very familiar songs. I am not too bad myself! It is, indeed great fun, if you haven't experienced it, you should try it!

Entertaining Others!

If you haven't guessed, I am a self-initiator. I love to make things happen. I like to make things happen for me first, but I truly enjoy making others enjoy their lives. The more I can make people happy, the better I like it. I must admit I like being the life of the party. I think the best thing you can do is motivate some one to have fun.

One challenge I had in this area is that my wife was not always ready for the work that goes with entertaining people. Nor did I realize how much work it takes to put on a simple party. I have learned that I can't always be as spontaneous due to the fact I am not the one who does the cooking or preparing of the food. But, I try to make sure I do a lot of the supporting stuff that needs to happen to make a great party come together. My wife has learned in order to live with me; she has to allow some of my spontaneity. We try to share the prep with our other members as much as possible.

One member of our Dash Club has a small young son and I have been known to go shopping to make sure we have all the toys needed to keep him happy when he visits. I call it being in training to be a grandfather. I believe I have as much fun playing with the toy trucks, blowing bubbles and flying toy helicopters as he does. I often see the joy on his mommy's face when she is getting a break and is able to talk to other adults, while I am on the floor for an hour or two setting up the dump truck site with him. All of this makes for good Dash interactions with other members.

I will guarantee you one thing, that if you become one who entertains others, you will often be one that gets entertained by others and this is total mutual satisfaction for all parties involved. This is good Dash work. I actually can't comprehend how people can be loners. But, if you are a loner, you should step out of your comfort zone and try entertaining a friend or two, it will change your Dash for ever.

Chapter 13

Dash Actions:

1. Leave the laptop home on your next vacation!
2. Only use your cell phone to make calls!
3. Give your employer 101% and nothing more!
4. Remember home is for regeneration and you will be more productive if you take time to rest and relax!
5. Leave your desk for lunch!
6. Take at least one coffee or drink break a day,two if you earn or deserve them!
7. Live for the weekend and don't let one go by with out great enjoyment!
8. Enjoy entertaining your friends!
9. Take long and great vacations as often as you can!
10. Stay home and recuperate if you are sick, it will be good for you and your colleagues!

Chapter 14

HOW CAN I HELP?

This is a question we all have to learn to ask ourselves over and over. During this writing a major tragedy befell the United Sates of America. My beloved hometown of Algiers in New Orleans, Louisiana was hit by the vicious hurricane called Katrina. I don't think any of us will ever forget the devastation that hit our precious, southern coastline. If you think I thought life was precious when I started writing this book, imagine what I think about life after having my mother call me from the New Orleans Hyatt Hotel and tell me she was riding out the storm there. Then imagine having one of my friends come to me with a picture of the Hyatt with all the windows blown out and asking me, "is this the hotel your mother told you she was going to be staying in during the storm." Two days later my mother called me from Baton Rouge, Louisiana and said everything was okay. I breathed a sigh of relief and I am still counting my blessings. All I could ask my mother was how could I help? My mother needed my moral support more than she needed money or things.

After this storm hit, I was glad to hear our Sr. Minister at church report that many people had called him and wanted to know how the church was going to help the victims of this horrific storm. I was also so glad to hear he had put plans in place to take all the money we collected in a certain fund that Sunday and give it to an agency that was already helping these victims. I contribute regularly to my church to meet various needs of the community. Our church takes every opportunity to help those less fortunate than ourselves.

A great part of making our Dashes long and lustrous is helping others every chance we get. Some of the most rewarding times in my life were when I was able to help a friend or family member in some way. I am thankful that I have had the opportunity and the resources to do this through moral, physical and financial support. My wife is even more giving than I am and this makes for a very giving family. We also try to encourage helping and giving in our friends and family members. The giving of our money is one thing, but the giving of ourselves and our time is truly remarkable.

On Being Charitable!

I use to be afraid to make myself an organ donor and have the sticker put on my driver's license. Then I was faced with the most unique situation of having my brother get very sick. It all started out with him catching the flu while on a trip visiting his in-laws in Oakland. To my understanding, the doctors said, the same virus that caused the flu attacked his heart muscles as well. He was diagnosed with congestive heart failure. His heart was damaged beyond repair. He ended up in the hospital for over a year, as they searched to find him a new heart. Then one day he got the call and he was immediately rushed to the hospital and given the heart of a nineteen year old man that had died in an accident in Denver. I viewed this event from my vantage point as another zero sum game. One person had to lose their life for another to live. My brother is still alive and well because of this tremendous donation. Very soon after this happened to my brother, I was at a conference and there were people there promoting the organ donor program. I proudly walked up and signed up for my donor sticker. Today, I wear my donor sticker proudly and encourage everyone I can to get one.

Often when we are faced with our own mortality, we don't know how to deal with it. The reason I had never gotten the card before was due to fear and lack of education on the subject. It was, as if, by putting that sticker on my card I was sure to die. Well guess what? I am surely going to die and so are you. But, we are alive and well today and living this life in a wonderful way and that is the agenda for today. Who knows what tomorrow will bring. But, understanding how precious it is to help others, makes living life all the better.

Giving to Others!

I am one that likes to share every aspect of my life with other people. I think I have been blessed beyond measures and I have way more than I need. I am now out to share all I can with as many people as I can. By helping others, I feel like my life is even more enhanced. When I witness the results of my giving to someone in need, my life is even greater. Every time I have stepped out of my comfort zone to help someone else I seem to receive more than I ever thought to give. Sometimes it manifests itself in small unique ways that can be so Dash enhancing.

I shared earlier about a trip I took to the Philippines and while I was there my heart went out to all the people begging on the streets. Now I must admit, when I am in the United States I am less likely to give your local beggar on the streets anything. From my experience working in city government, I know how much the local governments go out of their way to help the homeless. Most of our beggars in America only beg to get money to buy alcohol or drugs. They need help, but more than I can give them. On occasion I do roll down my car window and put a few coins in their hands. I usually tell them to go and eat and don't drink it away.

In the Philippines it is a different story. There is no welfare and there are no homeless shelters. The abject poverty is overwhelming in that country. When I see little children begging, it is hard to keep my hands out of my pocket. My local family there tells me don't give them any thing for fear they will follow you and keep begging. This is one of the few times when I don't listen to my family. I know their government doesn't provide for them. I give out pesos as if I have an endless source. I feel, if I can just help them a little, they are better off for at least that day, even though I know I am not solving the bigger problem.

I also over tip all the hotel support people. At the time of this writing a hundred pesos is equivalent to two US dollars. So I usually walk around with a roll of one-hundred peso bills and give them generously. The people serve you very well; I feel they deserve all I am willing to give.

What are we talking about here and how does this enhance the Dash? In the way of the Dash Club member, if we help some one, we are that much more enhanced in our lives. Life gets bigger and better when you know you have helped someone in some needed way. I think all aspects of our Dashes get a boost: our spirit, our health, our mental fitness, our well being, etc.

I have only sighted a few needs and opportunities to give, but there are many needs in your community and the rest of world that needs your help. I know I can't solve all the world problems. I do wish for the day when I truly have more money and resources than I know what to do with, I am sure I will give a lot of it to help others. I will be proud of all I do and I will be pleased with myself. This has got to be good for my Dash.

Prepare Your Children For A Great Life!

In my opinion, the true legacy of a life comes in what you can leave behind in your children. I know that our children don't always follow in our footsteps. I am one who believes you need to set up a framework for a good legacy. If your children choose to follow, they will bring about a great legacy that they can pass down to their children. If not, it is their loss not yours. One of the greatest examples of how to go about doing this was done by Earl Woods.

In 1996, I had the opportunity to walk the golf course with Earl. My family and I were a part of a small entourage that walked with him for several days. At one point in one of the days my daughter and I had him all to ourselves. He was a man that you would want to listen to for days. He was so full of wisdom and quite willing to share it. We were walking and watching his son make history in the third Amateur Open at Pumpkin Ridge Golf Course in Oregon. At the time, Earl was in the midst of writing "The Making of a Tiger." He shared with me and others that he had used golf to raise his son. He had used golf to teach him to think, to be disciplined, to have self-respect, to have respect for others, the ability to be a team player and many other principles we parents would like our children to incorporate into their lives. Needless to say, Earl built a strong legacy for his own life. I believe you all know the rest of this story. Tiger Woods is now the most famous athlete on the face of this earth at the time of this writing.

Needless to say, this encounter with Earl Woods was a great and rewarding experience for me and my family. Now you know where all those references to golf come from and why I live to take golfing vacations with my wife and family.

I won't sit here and tell you I have been madly successful preparing my children for life. I will tell you that they are both extremely healthy, thanks to my wife's cooking and God watching over them. At the time of this writing my daughter has just entered college and is working as a waitress to support that effort. My wife and I are also helping to support her while she is in school. She lives with several roommates who are also college students. My son is still trying to find himself. He still needs to complete high school and is also working and living on his own. I am very hopeful he will find himself and join his sister in the halls of higher learning soon. I am prepared to help him in every way I can.

You may remember from an earlier section of this book that I spent a lot of quality time with my children in their early years. I made sure they lived well and had great experiences. We took to them to church on a regular basis. Yes, I did preach at them on the challenges of life. My daughter has been heard saying, "He was very graphic when he was telling me how to handle boys." I am glad to say, she has handled herself fairly well with boys and I didn't need the proverbial father's "big stick" usually needed to keep boys away from their daughters during their formative years.

One thing I am most proud of is my wife and I was there

for our children during the time of their youth. I traveled a lot due to my job and career, but I made sure my toys and my play included them at all times. They both are decent golfers and can kick their fathers butt with a little practice on any given day. Their mother was and still is a great cook and they ate home cooked meals ninety percent of the time during their entire youth. They were one of the few kids in our upper middle class neighborhood who were not from a divorced home.

My wife and I were not by any stretch of the imagination perfect parents. I wanted to tell you before my kids let that cat out of the bag. I am not sure how my children will live out their lives, but I am sure they are both prepared to live great lives, if they so choose. I believe my wife and I did very well on understanding the basic needs of children and then we provided it. There were many times when we second guessed ourselves. Our kids had to deal with the cultural differences of an interracial marriage and that was often challenging when you add our strong personalities. These differences led to some parental confusion from time to time. Today, we say, we didn't do too badly.

I would hope, if you asked our children what did your parents do best to prepare you for the rest of your lives, they would answer, "they were great role models. Our parents love us and they demonstrated it all the time by their actions. They did what they said they were going to do and that was a good thing." Then, I would hope, that they would give you a great big smile that lingered on their face until you weren't looking at them anymore.

You may have noticed I have not tried to give you a lot of advice on exactly how to raise your children. I am more interested in sharing the experience and how it has always worked out for the better due to treating life as a most precious resource.

Chapter 14

Dash Actions:

1. Learn to give when ever you see a need!
2. Understand that there are needs to be met in your local community and through out the world!
3. Please give time to your children and build a lasting legacy, it will help them and make the world a better place!
4. Giving money is not the only way to solve a problem.
5. Giving of your time is very rewarding to the recipient and to you as the giver!
6. Be there when you are needed!

Chapter 15

SEX, ROMANCE AND LOVE!

Ah, the fun stuff and what I call the essence of life. Seriously, this goes along with food and water. First, I want to share a little bit of male perspective to the ladies and I would hope the men would agree with this tactic. If my wife and I were angry at each other and were going through the silent treatment phase of the argument, I would say to her, "Please don't cook me a meal if you are not going to take care of my other physical needs." There are three things that make me feel healthy in a given week. One is a good haircut, which my wife also provides from time to time. The second is a great evening meal, which my wife provides for me on a regular basis. The third is some passionate love making which happens on a weekly basis at this stage in our lives. But, when we are angry at each other, I still get the great meal and the hair cut, but the love making gets put on hold. Yes, there are two sides to every story and I am giving you mine, as a perspective and not as the one without blame. It takes two to argue and I am pretty good at my side of it. I share this because I believe this behavior puts marriages at great risk.

What I usually say to her is, "I can get a meal on almost any corner of our neighborhood." I have a barber that does a great job on my hair during these periods of disagreements. What I can't get is the sex, unless I am willing to violate my marriage vows, which I am not willing to do at this time. I believe my wife would tell you, "I can't get the intimacy that is needed for sex when I am angry at you." Many men find they need to violate their vows to fulfill this need rather than share how powerful this need is in their lives. Truth be told, men are often like dogs and when they can't get their physical needs met, they will look for it in other places. The withholding of sex by either party is probably the start of many failed marriages. I hope this initial discussion I have shared thus far gives the proper set up for the following Dash discussion.

Remember, my premise is that life is very precious and we should treasure and value every minute of it. We should do all we can to enjoy it. I think sex, romance and love is the icing on the cake. I also think, they are necessary experiences to keep people happy, content, and healthy. Although these experiences all go hand in hand, I believe for men, the most powerful is sex, due to its physical nature and far reaching consequences when not experienced properly.

Sex!

This is still going to be mostly a male perspective, ladies please forgive me, but I am just a mere man. Sex is one of the most wonderful things we can experience in life. It is the ultimate in fulfilling the need for two humans to touch each other. I have shared with friends, it is not just about the orgasm, and it is about the physical touching of skin, body and lips. It is about creating pleasure for your partner and yourself.

I do want to take a moment to share with you ladies something you may not know. I remember watching a movie call Sho-Gun back in the eighties. The Blackthorne character played by Richard Chamberlain was asked had he pillowed (had sex) since he arrived in Japan. He promptly answered, no. Mariko the character played by Yoko Shimada said, "This is not good, Lord Toranaga wants you to be healthy." I told you earlier how much I love to watch movies and this is a great one to rent for a great Dash enhancing weekend. What she was referring to was his physical health and the need to have his sexual, physical requirement met. Some of us men get physically sick if we do not have sex in a certain time period and for many men masturbation doesn't solve this problem. I have been told, it is not the same for most women. I do know some women going through menopause or on hormonal therapy have great sexual desires. I know we men can reduce it, too much, to just the physical act. I encourage you ladies to work hard to teach us how we can make it all work well for you and us.

Men I am not going to let you off the hook. I am of the premise that during sex, this is the time when you must be selfless, especially we men. I am also of the premise; if you seek to please your partner you will inevitably please yourself. My goal going into love making is to have my partner so pleased with what we are doing, she is overwhelmed with the physical pleasure she is experiencing. I want to do everything I possibly can to give her the ultimate pleasure for that time. I will not do anything that doesn't feel good to her, no matter how cool it feels to me. Hopefully, I learn enough from her about what she likes, that I can deliver it at the time she wants it. Also, remember I have been married for many years, if we haven't gotten it right by now shame on me and my wife. One more thing, we have got to be honest and truthful with each other, if we are going to get mutual benefit and not just be selfish.

Romance!

I will try to have this discussion from an intimacy point of view and hopefully, it will partially bail me out of the trouble I got myself into in the previous section. That same minister who was instrumental in inspiring me to the premise of this book gets credit for another Kodak moment. He shared with the church that his wife told him he was being romantic when he took time to wash the dishes or complete some other household chores. I must admit this was truly a time of learning for me. I felt very proud to find out how romantic I had become, since I started doing most of the household chores since our nest became empty – post children. I don't think my wife bought his take on romance and I think I need to have more discussion with his wife on what she was really trying to make him understand.

I don't think I am very romantic and I am always open to learning more, contrary to my wife's beliefs about me. I do bring home flowers from time to time and that results in a great big hug and smile from her. I set up great golfing weekends and jazzy encounters in some very classy hotels and resorts around the world, but I am not sure if I get romantic points for these activities. I don't ever remember my wife telling me you are very romantic when she came home and found all the clothes washed and folded. I usually get, how come you didn't take the sheets out of the dryer while they were still hot, when she sees them poorly folded and wrinkled. I just can't fold the sheets.

I think whatever romance is for you and your mate; it has to be a good thing. If I stick to Webster's definition of romance – 3. Imbued with idealism, a desire for adventure. 4. to be preoccupied with love or by idealizing love. 5. Expressing love or strong affection; I believe I am still in school on this topic and I have a lot to learn. I do offer that romance is something we all have to continue to pursue and try to bring to concrete action. I think women understand this state of being better than us men. I think women need to take the time to teach us men what they want in a romance.

Love!

I love the word "love." I think I understand its meaning fairly well. I love a lot of people and I love a lot of things. I think to be in love with a woman is the ultimate in self-actualization both emotionally and physically. I have been told I don't show a lot of emotion. (There is that struggle with romance again.) I think that it is the silly macho man in me that holds back the big emotional expression, like most men. I love to care for a woman. I like to do things for a woman. I love to take care of a woman. I like to give gifts to a woman. Again, from Webster we get – profoundly tender, passionate affection for another person, especially when based on sexual attraction. I also like the love for ones neighbor. I think if you experience the love of a soul mate for many years you have been blessed with a great life.

I understand this word to mean that I care about a person, place or thing. I love people! I love to be around them. I love to interact with them. I love to touch people physically and emotionally. I am careful not to let my love for people be abused. If you love people and are loved by people, you are experiencing an ultimate Dash.

In the vernacular of the Dash, love has got to be at the top of list, if we are going to have a truly dark and long Dash between our birth and death dates. It is all about loving one's self first, and then about loving life and finally about loving people. I really don't have anywhere else I want to take this. I think this discussion and understanding is the main ingredient for that icing on the cake from the perspective of enhancing your Dash. Finally, I believe love gives us the tool to measure the value of the relationship. If we can understand how valuable a loving relation is to us, we understand how much of ourselves it takes to meet the requirements of the relationship. Love is our meter for measuring that value.

Chapter 15

Dash Actions:

1. Understand that sex is one of the most important aspects to a healthy marriage for men!
2. Understand that intimacy for a woman is a very important part of having sex!
3. Continue to understand what it means to be romantic, especially you men, continue to study and explore it in every way you can!
4. Use love as the measuring stick for your relationships!
5. Continue to seek knowledge in all aspects of sex, romance and love!

Chapter 16

THE WORLD IS A WONDERFUL PLACE TO LIVE, WORK AND PLAY!

I have come to the conclusion that living in this world is a big series of experiences. Our lives are really all about the experiences we encounter in this world. It doesn't matter whether we are working, playing or whatever other aspects of living we are experiencing. In fact, I would say, our lives are made up of moving from one experience to the next. Yes, I am an eternal optimist and I love being one!

I once heard, if you studied a person's garbage, you would learn a lot about how they live their lives. I am one who believes you should enjoy taking out your garbage and understand what it represents as a part of your own life. You should work to enjoy all of the processes in your life (such as taking out your garbage) and understand how important they are to enhancing your Dash. But, on the other hand if you are fortunate enough to have the means to pay someone to take out your garbage – you should definitely enjoy that luxury. After taking out the garbage, which is usually kept in your garage, you should go and enjoy what is on the other side of your garage door – I believe that to be the rest of the world.

When I was young man, I was watching a show called, "Family" which starred Christy McNichols as Buddy and her brother was played by Willie Ames. I remember her mother on the show telling Buddy and her brother that they should not die until they had visited a place in the world that is at least three thousand miles away and on a foreign soil and the people speak a different language they had never heard. Now as a self-actuated adult, who now has traveled the world over, I fully understand what she was talking about.

I have spent time in many different countries around the world: starting from Vancouver, Canada to Baja, Mexico in North America; from Paris, France to Hanover, Germany in Europe; from Gotunda, Japan to Hobart, Tasmania in the Pacific Ocean. Each and every place afforded me nice memories of a unique and great experience. What is most interesting is how those memories continue to let me relive those great experiences in my life.

I remember the first time I woke up on the USS Enterprise in Subic Bay, Philippines at the tender age of 23. We had just left the beauty of Hawaii. I remember being totally excited that I was going to see a foreign country. I raced up to the hanger deck bounding two to three steps at a time. I then came up through the large door that provides access to the hanger deck and sped over to the plane elevator. The view was breath taking. The sky was the prettiest blue I had ever seen. It had a green tint from the beautiful palm trees. The air was full of very different smells. I learned later, it was a combination of the salt air from the Pacific Ocean, numerous smells of cooking from Olongapo City and a polluted river. The Sun was very hot and soft on my face.

The next thing I knew, I was in a taxi driving through a city that was about as festive as anything I had ever experienced. Remember, I am from New Orleans, Louisiana and I have experienced eighteen Mardi Gras Parties in New Orleans. We know festive when we see it. The people spoke a language that was a mixture of Spanish and Malaysian influence; it was called Tagalog.

"Magandang Umaga," which means "Good Morning," made for the first real foreign greeting I had encountered, other than the Spanish class I took in high school. The people were short and thin, with smooth brown skin and beautiful black hair.

The next country I visited was Hobart, Tasmania, Australia. The only thing I knew about Tasmania was from a cartoon that showed the Tasmanian devil spinning his way around and breaking everything in sight as he passed it. When I poked my head out of the hanger deck door this time, I was looking at a beautiful metropolis that looked a lot like Seattle, Washington at first glance. Here, I encountered a people that were White, European and young ladies who wanted to please you as much as they could and guys who wanted to kick your butt for messing with their young ladies. Ah yes, it was a fun time.

Talking about experiencing the world, I have been married for many years to a girl I met in the first foreign country I ever visited. In many ways I am still living that first world experience of visiting the Philippines. Things were truly beautiful at that time in my life and continue to be great for me today.

Aesthetic Arrest!

Definition – the action of stopping time with beauty or awe or sensationalism: Grabbing the attention. I am of the belief that we should experience this at least once a day. If you can't do it real time then you should have enough great experiences in your mind that will allow you to do at will, through your thought process and imagination.

Can you imagine seeing beauty that is so breath taking that it leaves you without words to describe it and at the same time it gives you a feeling of being totally blessed to have such a great privilege in your life. This happens when you see the Grand Canyon for the first five times. I am on number four and I will let you know if at number five it stops being a totally breath taking experience. Or seeing the Great Wall of China and expecting to see the tallest wall you have ever seen and instead seeing the longest set of steps in the world and understand, they were all built by people over many years of construction. I have been told that they are still being maintained by the same families that built them. A truly amazing thing to experience! Hopefully, the discussion above sets you up for the next section, because I think there are too many of us who don't cherish the time, when we are having these experiences. Please, continue to put yourself in situations that will allow you to experience aesthetic arrest and if you die from this type of arrest, you will have died a wonderful death.

You Have Got To Smell The Roses Today!

There are only so many times you are going to get to smell the roses. In many of the above Dash Actions I have encouraged you to do this at various times. In earlier sections, I have shared being on a trip through South Asia, while doing some of this writing. Here is the full account of that experience as I was writing this section.

I am literally sitting on a secluded Island called Bantayan, off the Coast of Cebu Island in the Bisayan Territory in the Philippine Islands. I am tucked inside of a cozy bamboo Nipa Hut looking at sandy white beaches with beautiful marine blue water with lovely, soft, gentle, rolling, waves. The sound of the surf is in the back ground and at the moment I can't hear any human voices. Oh, the place is called, The Ogtong Cave Resorts in the Santa Fe Barrio and it looks just like a place out of a great Pierce Brosnan, 007 movie. I am sure you get the picture. And none of this part of the vacation was planned.

How did I get here? We flew here to the Philippines on a planned vacation that included Singapore and then to the Philippines to find my wife's long lost relatives after many, many years. We were not sure what we were going to find when we set out on this vacation, but our good, long time friend booked us into this resort very near where my wife grew up in the Barrio of Maya in the Daanbantayan half of Cebu Island. This is where the roses come in - earlier today we drove into Maya and stopped an elderly lady who hid her mouth as she smiled lightly to hide her decaying and missing teeth. We asked her, if she knew my wife's family name. She not only knew their name, she was one of her long lost cousins. The reunion began. She asked my wife, "Are you the one who went to fisheries school?," and the crying began. We immediately convinced her to jump into the hired van and show us where the family was now living. She took us directly to a beautiful, colorful home that was owned by my wife's brother. We found my wife's family who had given up for dead.

Why hadn't my wife made this trip back to the Philippines much earlier in her life? I asked that question myself. I agree with part of her answer, that we did not have the workable finances to support such an effort in the earlier years. But, I also know we have always done anything we have wanted to do, once we put our minds to it. By the way, my wife did visit the Philippines three years after I married her and sent her back there as promised. For reasons that make some sense, but don't fully add up, she did not visit her home in the barrio of Maya. She said, she was afraid to go home. At that time the Philippines were experiencing a time of Marshal Law under the Marcos regime.

We have now discovered and reacquainted ourselves with about forty plus family members, many of whom were not even born when my wife left home the first time. I have never really been much of an uncle or a brother-in-law. I enjoyed this reunion more than I ever dreamed. I have discovered a cool nephew whom I hope to bring to the United States as soon as possible. I have some new nieces that are knock-outs to look at. I have also discovered many sister and brother-in-laws that I can't wait to spend more time getting to know.

Too many times we don't take the time to smell the roses or enjoy the beach or the other beautiful metaphors we use for enjoying life. The Maya experience has taught me to truly go after those things that can add so much more meaning to my life. And, oh what an enhancement it makes to your life long enjoyment of people.

I have made a big decision due to this experience. As I shared earlier, I have purchased a home on the sandy beach very near Maya. I will try to visit Maya no less than once a year to see if the fragrance of the roses gets better and better by continuing to visit and enjoy all of this new family we have found.

Chapter 16

Dash Actions:

1. Enjoy as much of this world as you can, it is a part of your life experiences!
2. Continue to put yourself in situations that take your breath away due to the beauty!
3. Enjoy every minute of a beautiful view or fantastic scenery or listening to great music!
4. Follow your first mind, it will take you to some interesting places!
5. Take time to smell the roses of today!

Chapter 17

ENHANCING YOUR DASH FOR MAXIMUM SUCCESS!

Remember, the Dash is a very short symbol, but it doesn't have to represent a very short and insignificant life! Yes, I know everything is relative. I think what is more important about living is making sure everything you do to live is relevant and gives your life great and wonderful meaning.

Prepared For Life!

Here are some interesting question. When are we prepared to live? Once we are prepared to live, how much do we get to change or enhance the way we live? In the first chapter of the book I talked about your birthday. I told you this was the first day of the rest of your life. Again, I want to tell you that everyday after that is also the first day of the rest of your life. Every day is a day to live and every day is a day to prepare to live and enjoy the next day. Are we ever prepared for life? Or is it living life itself that prepares us to live the rest of our lives? It is fun to play with words in this manner, but what makes it more fun is to know that I can control where life is taking me and when I lose that control; I am unprepared for what happens next. I promise you I will join you in finding that place where life just keeps getting better and better.

Finding the Sweet Spot!

In most of the things we do in sports, we are always looking for the place where we will perform our best. I have heard people say, he is in the zone when referring to Michael Jordan or Michelle Wie or my favorite athlete, Tiger Woods. I believe this zone is referred to as when these athletes' performance is at their best and that peak performance leads to winning.

I have heard people say, she or he is peaking in their career. She closed a million dollar deal in Asia last week, she is sure to be vice president by the end of the year. He just wrapped up another one and he is already headed to Europe to close the third one. We have many of these metaphors to refer to people performing at their best.

I think in life there is a time when you are "living life as well as you can" and I call this the "Sweet Spot." This is a place and time where it has all come together for you and yours. This may not necessarily be when you are the richest you can be or the healthiest you can be. This may not be the time when you have accomplished all that you are going to accomplish. This may be early in life before you have made your fortune or it may be a time when you are done with your career and retired.

In the Dash way of things, this is the time when life is great and you wouldn't have it any other way. It is a time when you have things under total control. This is a time of joy, peace and happiness. This is the "Sweet Spot." Get there soon!

Retirement in Perspective!

Many of us focus a lot of time, effort and resources on

retirement. This should not be to the detriment of your Dash. If you spend a lot of time putting away money and resources before you have spent enough on making your life enjoyable, you are dimming your Dash. You may be making a bigger sacrifice then you need to at this particular time in your life. Many people stop enjoying life to focus on preparing for retirement for fear they won't have enough resources to retire on. It would be a very sad day if you raised the million dollars for retirement and you died the next day and left it all to your kids. My mother loves to tell her children, "I am spending your inheritance, so be sure you put something away for your own rainy day."

Too many of us live for the day we will retire. Again, I believe true retirement is to stop going to a place that someone else has invested in to have you make money for them. If you are working for someone else, you are building up their retirement faster than you are building up your own. Remember, you are reading a book written by someone who has had two failed business before understanding that his true passion is to write. Thank you for buying this book and helping me to continue to live out my dream.

In the Workable Finance chapter above I gave you some tips and hints on how to make sure you will have the finances you need to retire. Now I am trying to talk you into keeping retirement in perspective. I am encouraging you to think of retirement as a goal to truly do what you want to do in life, while you are still vibrant enough to enjoy it.

Aging Gracefully!

I have a buddy that at the time of this writing was about

seventy-two years old. He was once asked, "What do you do for a living?" He smiled and replied with great enthusiasm, "Nothing and I am very good at it!"

If you ever had the opportunity to meet him, you would come away with a great, positive experience. I always enjoy being with him and he has never missed a chance to share some information with me that he thought would enhance my life. He is what I picture as growing older gracefully. Notice, I didn't use the term "old." My buddy is not old, in fact, I am twenty years younger than him and I am the old man in relative comparison. He is busy and active living life on the coast of Southern California. He starts with a daily routine; he works out at the gym every other day with men twenty to thirty years his junior. He golfs at least twice a week and works at a golf course as a marshal at least twice a week. I want to get to that plateau as soon as I can. I think I will never stop writing and retirement for me will be living in that house in the Philippines on those sandy white beaches cranking out novels for part of the year. The rest of the times I will be here in Arizona selling those novels and playing golf with a great lady.

Chapter 17

Dash Actions:

1. Live for this day first and then prepare for the rest of your life!
2. Find that sweet spot in life where it doesn't get much better for you!
3. Retire in style!
4. Grow old gracefully, but not feebly!
5. Play a lot of golf or what ever other thing you like to do, every chance you get!

Chapter 18

DEATHDAY!

Well, in all of the pages above we have tried to share enough information to allow you to see your deathday as the natural conclusion to your life. In fact, if this book has been successful at describing how important it is to enjoy the journey to the end of your Dash, your Deathday is just one last big action, that you never see coming. I hope that every day you walk on this earth you will be blessed beyond belief. Hopefully, by now you are smiling and trying to figure out what is the next fun thing you are going to do now that you have read such an inspiring book. I hope by now you should have a better attitude and no matter what situation you find yourself in, you have decided "it's all good!" Please make the most out of your life, did you hear me? I am begging you to please make the most of your life and by the time you are done, it will be easy to write that final date: A day that will go down in your personal history as a good day.

The deathday will simply be another day in your life that will mark the day a great life ended and everyone who experienced you will have great memories that they will carry in their hearts long after your deathday has passed. This is the end of this book, but not the end of my Dash. I think I will get on with it!

As Worf from the Klingon Empire would say "it is a good day to die!" But, I do hope it is a long time coming for you and yours. And to borrow another saying from Star Trek, Mr. Spock would say, "Live long and prosper!"

DASH ASSESSMENT SURVEY

This is a tool for helping you assess how you are doing in the progression of creating a great Dash.

Instructions:
To achieve a simple portrayal of the progress of your Dash, answer the questions with out much contemplation and add up your points. Less than 100 points you need to reassess you life. Be honest with yourself!

1. **Do you like yourself?**
   a. A lot - 15
   b. Enough - 10
   c. Too much – 5
   d. Not much – 1

2. **How much time do you spend on your personal improvement?**
   a. Too much – 15
   b. Not much – 5
   c. Too little – 1
   d. About right – 10

3. **How often do you take time to reflect on how important life is to you?**
   a. Often - 10
   b. Too Often - 15
   c. Some - 5
   d. Not at all – 1

Continue on Next Page

4. **How often do you take time to smell the roses?**
   a. Not at all – 1
   b. Often – 10
   c. Every day – 15
   d. Occasionally – 5

5. **How much do you work at your profession or vocation?**
   a. 50% - 5
   b. 100% - 15
   c. 125% - 1
   d. 75% - 10

6. **How much of your vacation do you use in a year?**
   a. Some of it – 5
   b. Very little – 1
   c. All of it - 10
   d. Go in the hole – 15

7. **How much time do you spend with family and friends?**
   a. A lot - 10
   b. Enough - 5
   c. Too much – 15
   d. Not enough – 1

8. **How much do you pay attention to your health?**
   a. A lot - 10
   b. Enough - 5
   c. Too much – 15
   d. Not enough – 1

9. **Do you have workable finances?**
   a. A lot - 10
   b. Enough - 5
   c. More than enough – 15
   d. Not enough – 1

10. **Do you believe in something for spiritual purposes?**
    a.   Yes - 10
    b.   Very much - 15
    c.   Hardly at all - 1
    d.   A little - 5

BOOK ORDER FORM

MANAGEMENT ASPECTS COMPANY
1355 S. Corrine Drive, Suite 101
Gilbert, AZ 85296
Phone: 480-718-5785
orders@managementaspects.com
www.managementaspects.com
www.thedashclub.com

The Dash Club   **- $14.95**
Black Experience, Strategies and Tactics in the Business World
      - $19.95
For My Peoples   **- $13.95**
May I Help You Understand?   **- $16.95**
The Mahogany Table   **- $24.95**

Requestor's Information:

Name:_____

Address:_____

City:_____

State:_____

Zip_____

Quantity:_____   Amount: $_____

Method of Payment:

Check_____   Visa _____   MasterCard _____

Card Number:_____